THE STORY OF
Buffalo Bill

"Buffalo Bill is, from spur to sombrero, one of the finest types of manhood this country has ever produced."

— CURTIS GUILD

*Riding the Pony Express was such fun that Bill
hardly thought about danger*

Weekly Reader Books presents

THE STORY OF
Buffalo Bill

By EDMUND COLLIER

Illustrated by NICHOLAS EGGENHOFER

ENID LAMONTE MEADOWCROFT

Supervising Editor

PUBLISHERS Grosset & Dunlap NEW YORK

For

My Mother

This book is a presentation of Weekly Reader Books.
Weekly Reader Books offers book clubs for children
from preschool through high school. For further
information write to: **Weekly Reader Books,**
4343 Equity Drive, Columbus, Ohio 43228.

Published by arrangement
with Grosset & Dunlap.
Weekly Reader is a trademark of Field Publications.
Printed in the United States of America.

The Story of Buffalo Bill

Contents

[*v*]

Illustrations

[*vii*]

ILLUSTRATIONS

THE STORY OF
Buffalo Bill

Over one shoulder he had slung a quiver of arrows

CHAPTER ONE

Show Boy

THE boy standing in the farmhouse door-way looked like an Indian. He wore a head-dress of long turkey feathers. The tail of the headdress streamed down his back almost to the ground.

Over one shoulder he had slung a quiver of arrows. In his hand was a homemade bow. His brown eyes were keen. His face was tanned. He was straight-backed and strong for his age.

But he wasn't an Indian. He was seven-year-old Bill Cody. He was a lad who would some day become famous, so famous that a letter with only his picture on it would reach him anywhere in the world.

Bill couldn't know that now, however. He was waiting in the doorway for his sisters to finish their breakfast and come out to play their favorite game of Indians.

It was a bright spring morning. Crows were cawing in the woods. A deer was feeding warily on the edge of a sunny meadow. Bill's eyes sparkled as he watched these things and planned the day's adventures.

The family's huge black dog, Turk, came out and stood beside him. Turk was a powerful animal and a great hunter. He whined. He was getting impatient.

Bill was, too.

"Hurry up!" he shouted to his sisters. "If you don't hurry, I won't wait for you."

Helen, the youngest, was dawdling over her breakfast. Lydia was helping their mother put up sandwiches.

Lydia shouted back, "Shut up, Willie! I'm making your lunch. If you don't wait, you won't get any."

Bill's black-bearded father, Isaac Cody, came outside. He began to fill his pipe while he waited for thirteen-year-old Sam. He and Sam had already milked the cows before breakfast.

"What show are you putting on today, youngster?" Mr. Cody asked Bill.

"Wagon train and Indians," Bill told him. "The girls will be the wagon train. I'll raid them."

"You sure make those kids step around, don't you, boy?" Isaac said, chuckling.

Sam came out and went off with his father to their day's plowing. Bill went down to the barn to help them harness the team.

Soon Lydia and Helen came down, carrying their dolls and the lunch basket. Bill took com-

[5]

mand. They started off on a trail through the woods. It led toward the Mississippi River, which flowed near their Iowa farm. Turk followed along.

They came to a high place that looked out over open hilly fields. Bill stopped them.

"You're a wagon train of settlers, heading West," he explained. "I'm Indians. I have to find you. When you see me, you have to pull your wagons into a circle. Like a fort. I'll attack you. Take Turk."

Bill watched the girls head out over the fields. Turk bounded along ahead of them. He made side trips after rabbits. But he never got too far off to protect the children.

Soon Bill sneaked off into the woods. He made a wide circle. His plan was to get in front of the make-believe wagon train. Then he would hide and surprise it.

After a while he came out on a hill above the river. Below him on a flat place was a group of tepees—a village of the friendly Fox Indians.

Bill saw three slim Indian boys leave the village. He knew they went to a mission school, and could speak a little English. They were about Bill's age. As they came up the hill toward him, he lay down behind a log and watched them glide silently by.

Bill waited till they were almost out of sight. Then he got up and followed. He tried to keep behind trees so they wouldn't see him. Once the rear Indian stopped and looked back.

Bill froze. Soon the Indian boy went on again. "This is real scouting," Bill thought. He had almost forgotten his sisters.

The Indians were climbing a long hill. They rounded the top of the hill and dropped out of sight. As Bill came near the hilltop he went to his knees. He crawled through the trees.

When he came to the edge of the hill, he flattened out on his stomach and looked over. No Indians!

Bill lay there searching the slope with his eyes. The woods thinned toward the foot of the hill. Beyond were the fields.

After a while Bill spied something yellow. The girls' lunch basket! It was hidden in a big rock pile. Bill could see only the handle and part of the rim. Where were Turk and the girls? Bill could hear the gurgle of a creek. Perhaps his sisters had grown tired of waiting for his attack and had gone wading.

Something moved close to the rock pile. Bill stiffened and strained his eyes. One by one he made out all three Indians. They were lying flat among the leaves. Only a sharp eye could have seen their brown bodies at all.

One was slithering like a snake toward the rock pile. He came in full sight on the rocks. He stretched out an arm, and pulled the basket loose. Then the three Indians came sneaking back up the hill.

Bill's heart was beating fast. He reached into his quiver for a blunt arrow, fitted it to his bowstring, and waited. The enemy was not thirty feet away when he rose suddenly to one knee.

The Indians stopped, surprised. Bill let out a shrill whistle. He yelled, "Turk! Help! Turk! Help!"

Then he aimed carefully at the middle of the boy who was carrying the basket. The bow-

[*8*]

string twanged. The feathered arrow sped straight. It hit the Indian hard. He dropped the basket and doubled over.

Far away by the creek, Turk was barking.

The other two Indian boys started for Bill. There was a stout hickory stick beside him. His fist closed around it. The Indians rushed in.

Bill came to his feet. He swung the stick. It caught one boy on the shoulder. He stumbled and went down.

The other attacker grappled with Bill. Arms and bodies locked, they wrestled. The Indian was the taller. He got a foot behind Bill's heel and over they went, Bill underneath.

[9]

A black streak shot up the hill. The Indian who had been hit with the arrow saw it. He shouted a warning. The boy on top of Bill looked over his shoulder.

He jumped off. But before he could stand up, Turk hit him and bowled him over. The huge black dog twisted around. Growling, he faced the Indians. His white teeth showed under a curling lip.

All three Indian boys were on their feet. They watched the fierce dog tensely—scared but too proud to show it.

"Quiet, Turk," Bill ordered.

The dog stopped growling.

Bill had an idea. What a show this would be! His eyes glowed.

"You're my prisoners," he said clearly to the Indians. "You—" he pointed to the one he had hit with the blunt arrow—"get my arrow."

The Indian boy obeyed. Bill told another to pick up the lunch basket. Then he marched them down the hill. Turk, at their heels, made sure they didn't run away.

They came near the rock pile. Suddenly the

[*10*]

girls popped out from behind it. They had followed Turk up from the creek.

They were wide-eyed. Half-scared, half-curi-
ous.

"Bill! Bill!" they shrieked. "What happened?"

Bill stopped the parade. He straightened up
proudly and pointed his bow at the captives.

"These warriors," he said seriously, "broke
the treaty. They went on the warpath. They
attacked your wagon train. They stole your
provisions—"

"Oh, Bill—" Lydia interrupted.

Bill paid no attention. He went on talking.

"I am a friendly chief. I am Good Heart,
chief of the Pawnees. I have brought back your
supplies. I have brought back the thieves."

Little Helen was still wide-eyed. She felt the
spirit of the game along with Bill.

But Lydia, older, said, "Oh, stop it, Bill! I
bet these Indian boys are hungry. Let's share
our lunch with them."

Bill broke into peals of laughter. "Just what
I was going to do, Liza," he said.

[*11*]

The scared Indian boys loosened up. Their faces became all smiles.

Presently all six—brown and white—were sitting peacefully on the rock pile. The lunch was vanishing.

"Bill," Lydia asked, "why do you always play-act everything?"

Bill stopped short with a sandwich halfway to his mouth. He looked hard at Lydia. His eyes were bright with the idea that had come to him.

"When I'm grown up," he said, "I'm going to be a showman. I'm going to run my own show!"

CHAPTER TWO

Sam

ALL afternoon they played. Bill invented one game after another. Finally, as the sun swung down the west, they'd had enough. The Codys said good-by to their Indian friends. Tired, and hungry again, they headed back to the farmhouse.

When they arrived their mother was cooking supper. They surrounded her, pulled her head down, and pretended to scalp her.

"Help! Help!" she screamed, laughing.

The corn dodger in the oven started burning. She pushed the children away, and rescued it just in time.

"Mercy me! Will you wild Indians settle

down and wash up?" Mary Ann Cody scolded gently.

Sam came into the kitchen. His boots were muddy. His face was burned and dusty.

"Father'll be late," he said. "He wants to finish plowing the new field."

Soon they were settled at the table. Their

mother gave them a steaming hot meal. There were crisp corn dodgers. There was fried pork. There were quarts of applesauce and gallons of fresh milk.

The five ate hungrily. Bill and the girls told their mother about the Indians.

"I don't know that I want you playing with those savages," she said doubtfully.

"But, Mama, they're nice," Helen piped.

"They're fun," Bill said.

Sam pushed back from the table. "I'm going for the cows," he told them.

"Can I go too, Ma?" Bill asked.

"*May I?* Not, *can I?*" his mother corrected.

Mary Ann Cody had once been a school-teacher. She wanted her children to speak good English.

"Yes, you may go. Sam's tired. He'll be glad of help."

"You can come if you help milk," Sam said.

Bill jumped up from the table. He'd do anything for a chance to ride. They went down to the stable. Sam threw a saddle on Betsy Baker. Betsy came of racing stock, and she was nervous. Sometimes she behaved badly. But Sam liked to ride her because she was so fast.

Bill got up bareback on a slow old horse. He wasn't allowed to ride any but the gentlest. He'd ridden ever since he was big enough to straddle a saddle. He knew he could ride as well as Sam, but at seven that didn't count.

They rode out of the barnyard, Turk trotting after them. He was a great help on this

[*15*]

job. If he had been able to open the gates, he could have driven the cows alone.

Betsy Baker went skimming over the fields like a bird. Bill's old horse came lumbering far behind. Turk scared up a meadow lark.

Some of the cows were lowing at the pasture gate. They wanted to be milked. Sam opened the gate and they streamed through. They headed for home of their own accord.

But yearling calves, and cows that were not giving milk, were hiding out. It was almost dark. Sam could see the stray cows moving like shadows through the alders that lined the creek.

He sent Turk down to get them. The dog's yipping quickly sent the beasts plunging into the open.

By this time Bill had caught up. Sam sent him to comb the upper slope, where more cows were hiding behind big clumps of high-bush blueberries. As Bill came down, one of the cows he was driving loosened a rock. It went bounding down the hill.

It rolled near Betsy Baker, and she started to prance. Then she began to run. As Sam tried to stop her, she reared up on her hind legs. Twice

[*16*]

As Sam tried to stop her, she reared up on her hind legs

she went up. The third time Bill thought she was going over. But Sam brought the butt of his quirt down on top of her head.

"No, you don't, Betsy!" he told the mare. Her front feet came down hard.

Bill and Turk drove the cattle through the gate. Sam followed, still trying to quiet the mare.

As he reached down to shut the gate, Betsy reared up again. Sam was sitting loosely in the saddle. As she went up he grabbed at her mane. The mare hurtled over backward.

Bill heard the commotion. As Betsy went over, he turned and pounded back as fast as the old horse could go. Sam had been pinned under Betsy's saddle.

Betsy Baker had scrambled to her feet. But Sam was lying still on the ground. Bill jumped off his horse. He knelt beside his brother.

"Sam! Sam!" the frightened boy shouted.

Turk was beside him, whining.

Sam lay still. He did not answer.

Bill stood up. Betsy Baker had caught her foot in the reins. She was standing still. Bill looked at his own horse. Then he looked at Betsy. What he wanted now was speed.

Jaws tight, Bill walked over to the mare. He untangled her foot from the reins, and climbed into the saddle.

Forgetting danger, he slammed his heels into the mare's ribs. Luckily, the mare went flying across the field to where Isaac Cody had been plowing.

He was just starting home with his team and wagon. Bill stuttered out his fearful story. His father wasted no words.

"Bring the wagon," he said tensely.

He jumped down and was on Betsy almost before Bill got off.

Bill climbed into the wagon and slapped the work horses with the ends of the reins till they broke into a gallop. The wagon went rattling and jolting across the fields.

When they reached the pasture gate, his father was waiting there, holding Sam in his arms.

Isaac Cody gently placed his oldest son in the wagon bed.

[*19*]

"Is he—is he—?" Bill began.

"Sam's dead, boy," Isaac told him. His voice was hollow.

Bill's horse had gone home. Isaac tied Betsy to the back of the wagon. He climbed onto the seat beside Bill. The boy lifted the reins and the team started off.

Turk, who had stayed with Sam, walked behind, his head hanging.

Isaac Cody sat slumped and quiet. At last he said, with a choke in his voice, "Willie, how can I tell his mother?"

CHAPTER THREE

The Born Marksman

IT WAS a sad time for the Cody family after Sam's death. One evening after the children had gone to bed, Mr. and Mrs. Cody were sitting in the kitchen.

Isaac was reading the Bible aloud, when he noticed that Mary Ann was crying.

"There, now, Mother," he said comfortingly. "I know it's hard, but—"

"I just can't stand it any longer, Isaac," she interrupted. "Everywhere I look around this farm, I see my boy. I can't stand it! We've got to move."

Except for the cat purring under the old wood stove and the clock ticking on the shelf over the table, the room lay in dead quiet.

[*21*]

Thoughts were racing through Isaac's head.

"Ann," he said finally. "I've been thinking about moving for a long time. You know my brother Elijah, who moved to Missouri? He's doing fine with his store in Weston. I think we'd do better ourselves, though, if we went a mite farther west."

"Where would we go?"

"Kansas!" Isaac said with a ring in his voice. "It's going to be opened up soon for settlement. The Government is going to give 160 acres free to every settler. Weston is just across the river. You and the girls can stay with Lije till we get a place ready."

Mary Ann thought for a while. Then she said, "How about the children's schooling?"

"There'll be schools in Kansas soon enough," Isaac answered. "As for Bill, he doesn't like the smell of chalk dust anyway. A year away from school won't hurt him."

"Perhaps you're right," Mary Ann agreed. "All right. We'll go."

Bill was wild with excitement when he heard the news next morning. He couldn't wait to get off. And he was in the thick of all the preparations.

Isaac sold the farm and all the stock except enough mules and horses to move with.

He bought three huge boat-shaped wagons called prairie schooners. These covered wagons were long and strong. They were built especially for pioneers who were moving West.

The Codys loaded the prairie schooners with their furniture. They also loaded in as much farm equipment as they would need, and food for the trip.

At last they were ready to go.

Bill's mother and sisters rode in a large family carriage, varnished and polished till it shone. It was drawn by a span of fine horses in silver-mounted harness. The womenfolks found it much more comfortable than the springless covered wagons.

The caravan set out. Mr. Cody took two extra drivers. Bill appointed himself an armed escort for the wagons. He rode proudly along on his pony, with his rifle slung across the pommel of his saddle. The dog Turk followed.

[*23*]

It was a thirty-day trail from LeClair to Weston. But during the first part of the journey, the Codys were able to stop every night with settlers.

As they went on, though, the homesteads

were farther and farther apart. At last they saw no more. This pleased Bill. He whispered to his sisters, "I heard Father tell Mother we'll have to camp out tonight. Now we'll have some fun!"

But before it was time to camp, they came to a big river. Isaac Cody knew that it would take two trips to ferry the whole outfit over. He sent Bill across on the first trip with his mother and sisters, and told him to pick out a campsite. Bill was proud to be given this responsibility.

The boy found a spot near a brook where the water was clear enough to drink. Taking command of the other children, he got wood gathered, and a fire going. It was blazing before his father got over with the rest of the outfit.

Then Bill decided to go into the woods and kill some meat. Riding his pony and with the black dog nosing the ground ahead, he set out. Turk was good at trailing any kind of game. He soon found a deer in a thicket. Bill saw it jump out. He put the gun to his shoulder. But

[25]

his hand shook so much that he could not aim. He had buck fever. This often happens to a person the first time he has to kill something.

Turk came back and sat on his haunches in front of the boy. He looked disgusted. Bill had let his good hunting go to waste. But they went on, and the next time Bill was ready.

Turk followed a trail into another thicket. Bill rode around to the other side. He got there just as a small doe leaped out. Bill aimed at a spot just behind the animal's shoulder. He squeezed the trigger. The deer fell, shot through the heart.

[26]

Bill dragged the game onto a bank. He led his pony under it. After a hard struggle he managed to load the deer behind his saddle. Bursting with pride, he rode toward camp.

But his adventures for that day were not ended. Turk had run off after Bill had shot the doe. Now Bill heard Turk bark. It sounded as though the dog were calling for help. Bill dug his spurs into the pony.

He came to the edge of a clearing. On the other side he saw his two sisters, Lydia and Helen, who had come looking for him. They were behind a log, with their backs to their brother. And they were stiff with fright. Turk stood in front of them, barking fiercely. Suddenly his bark changed to a deep growl.

Bill saw a slinking yellow creature slide out of the woods—a big panther. It crouched. Then it sprang forward. Turk leaped at the same time. His strong jaws closed on the panther's throat.

Bill slid off his pony, with his rifle in his hand. He tried to aim at the beast, but it was thrashing about trying to break Turk's grip.

Bill couldn't shoot without hitting the dog.

The panther was powerful. Its muscles were as tough as whip leather. With a great twist, it threw the dog against the log. Turk lay there

stunned. The panther crouched again, ready to spring on Lydia and Helen, who were too frightened to run. Bill's gun roared. The panther was hit in mid-leap. It dropped to the ground snarling. Turk was up and on him. By the time Bill reached it, the beast was dead.

At this point, Isaac Cody, who had heard the shot, came bursting across the clearing. He was riding bareback on one of the wagon mules.

[28]

His face was pale even in the red light of the setting sun. He wiped cold sweat from his forehead. "Well, lad," he said, a catch in his voice. "I reckon there's two men in the family—again."

Bill was still too frightened to be proud. He

was also puzzled. The panther and the deer were the first big game he'd ever killed. He'd shot them both on the leap. How had he done it? As he led his pony back to the camping place he wondered about this.

Bill Cody did not know that he was a born marksman. He never dreamed that the time would come when thousands of people would marvel at the way he could shoot.

CHAPTER FOUR

Bill Takes a Trip

THE Codys had no more narrow escapes on the trip to Weston. There, they settled with Isaac's brother, Elijah. Isaac was anxious to get ready for the Codys' next move, to Kansas. He couldn't take his family to Kansas until the Government opened up the land for settlement. But he decided that he would go ahead, find a place to live, and start a trading post.

After breakfast, one morning, he talked this over with Bill's mother. The girls were washing the dishes. Bill leaned on the table beside his father.

"Elijah's making good money, trading with the Potawatomi Indians," he said. "I figure I can kill two birds with one stone. I'll take a load of trade goods across the river, and trade with the Indians while I build a house."

"It's dangerous, Isaac," his wife said. "Where do you plan to settle?"

"There's no one trading with the Kickapoo Indians along Salt Creek," Isaac replied. "And that's not far west of Leavenworth."

"Can I go with you, Father?" Bill put in eagerly.

"Oh, no!" Bill's mother exclaimed quickly.

"There, there, now, Mother," said Isaac. "It's not really dangerous. Fort Leavenworth is full of soldiers. And the Indians are friendly now."

"All kinds of dreadful things could happen," Mrs. Cody said. "I—"

"But, Mother, I want to go!" Bill broke in. "It'll be fun!"

Isaac said, "The boy's got to learn to do a man's work, Ann. I can use him handling the logs for the cabin. It's a two-man job."

So, a few days later, Bill and his father loaded one of the prairie schooners with things the Kickapoos would like. There were bolts

[*31*]

It seemed to Bill that all the world was rolling West

of bright red calico. There were boxes of colored beads. There were mirrors, hunting knives, vermilion dye, tobacco. There were cast-iron pots and kettles.

When all was ready, they said good-by to Mrs. Cody and the girls, who were to stay with Uncle Elijah.

Isaac held the reins over six fine mules. Bill sat next to him, with his rifle ready in case he saw a chance to shoot some fresh meat.

As they started out, a tired wedge of north-bound geese flapped across the pink sunrise. They went honking down to rest and feed on the Missouri River. It wasn't long till the sun grew gold in the soft spring sky.

At the ferry, Bill and his father joined a long line of travelers. It seemed to Bill that all the world was rolling West.

They pounded across the gangplank onto the boat. The smell of muddy water was mingled with the odors of livestock and leather. Bill was bouncing with excitement at the sight of the long-haired plainsmen clad in fringed buckskin. The look of distances was in the plainsmen's friendly eyes. They held their long rifles lovingly in their firm hands. In his heart the boy felt that some day he would be a plainsman, too.

Now Bill and his father left the "Big Muddy" behind. They headed for Fort Leavenworth, which was a great army post on the edge of the frontier. There they stopped for lunch. The blare of bugles and the drilling of blue-clad cavalry sent little tingles running up and down Bill's back.

Out of Leavenworth, they drove along the well-marked Salt Lake Trail. This was the highroad to the West. Three miles beyond the fort, they passed a trading post which was doing a lively business. It belonged to a man named Riveley.

Beyond that the traffic began to thin out. The faster wagons pulled ahead and others turned off the road.

The sun climbed higher and the day grew warmer. Bill got to thinking about their moving, and the why of it.

"Father," he asked, "why can't we bring the

[*34*]

whole family into Kansas and settle right now?
Why do we have to wait for Congress to pass a
law or something?"

"It's kind of hard to explain, lad," replied
his father. "I don't know if you can understand it."

"Yes, I can."

"Well, you know that in the South, folks
have big plantations. They have slaves to work
them. They figure they couldn't do without
them. Up North the states have passed laws
against slavery. They claim it's wrong to have

[35]

slaves. Besides, they don't really need them.

"Now the states were gradually getting rid of slavery anyway. But then new land was opened up. The North didn't want any slavery in the new land. The Southerners wanted to bring in their slaves. The argument got pretty hot for a while.

"About thirty-five years ago they worked out an agreement called the Missouri Compromise. It divided the land up pretty fairly. Now the country's got a lot more new land.

"Some people want Congress to let the settlers in Kansas vote whether they'll be slave or free. If Congress lets them do that, each side will send as many settlers as it can to Kansas before voting day.

"Right now there are a lot of badmen gathered across the river in Missouri. They aim to come over here and make Kansas vote to be a slave state."

"How can they?" asked Bill.

"Guns, my boy. Guns and knives. They aim to control the vote by force."

"Which side are you on, Father?"

"I'm against slavery, my boy, in any form. In this country *every* man has a right to be a *free* man."

"Are we going to get into fights with the border badmen?"

"I surely hope not."

This was Bill's first lesson in politics. It kept his mind busy till his father stopped the wagon at the top of a long hill. The mules needed a rest.

Isaac pointed with his whip down into the grassy valley below them. It was a peaceful place. A stream ran through it. Its green slopes rose gently to patchily forested hills.

"There it is," Isaac said. "There's Salt Creek Valley. Isn't she pretty?"

[*37*]

"You bet," Bill agreed. "Where are the Indians?"

"Not far off, boy. You'll see plenty of them. The Kickapoo Reservation is close by. Soon as they know we're setting up a trading post, they'll come flocking in.

"Straight west over the next ridge of hills is prairie. Nothing but prairie, and then desert. This is where we're going to settle. Let's go, mules."

Isaac picked up the lines and the white-topped wagon started down the hill toward their new home.

CHAPTER FIVE

The Spotted Pony

———————————————

THEY came to a lightly wooded flat by the river. Bill's father handed the lines to his son and got down. He pulled a shovel from the back of the wagon, thrust it deep in the ground. He turned over a shovelful of sod.

He picked up a handful of dirt and rubbed it between his fingers. It was rich and black and crumbly.

"Great!" Isaac said. "This looks like a perfect spot. Get down, boy. This is home. Water, wood, and good deep soil! What more can a man ask for?"

They unhooked the mules. and set up their tent. Then they fixed places for a cookfire and a campfire.

That night, after a good meal, they were sitting drowsily in front of the warm flames, when Bill heard a far-off rumbling bellow.

"What's that?" he asked.

"Buffalo," his father told him. "From here on west, there are plenty of them."

Next morning they set to work. Isaac chopped down the trees. Bill dragged them up to the house site with the mules, and notched the ends so the logs would fit tight.

The Salt Lake Trail ran right in front of the place where they were putting the house. The sun wasn't very high before Bill looked up to see a stagecoach coming down the steep hill into the valley.

The six mules which were pulling it broke

into a run as the driver let off the brake at the foot of the hill. Bill noticed the armed guards riding on top.

The coach was painted bright red and green. There were pictures on the door panels. Not a squeak came from the well-oiled wheels.

As the stage spun gaily by, the passengers shouted greetings, and the driver cheerily waved his whip.

From then on, there was never a dull moment for Bill. There was always something new to watch. Prairie schooners drawn by long strings of oxen plodded by. The children in the westbound wagons yelled at him as they passed. Cavalrymen from the fort often stopped to visit. Prospectors, scouts, guides, traders, trappers filled Bill's mind full of dreams of the Far West.

And the Codys hadn't been there a full day before Kickapoo Indians appeared.

When the Indians learned there was trading to be done, they came every day. Often they brought their children along.

The Kickapoos were good neighbors. Bill

[*41*]

soon made friends with the boys. Often he would stop work to play with them. These bronzed boys were straight, strong, and very athletic.

Bill learned their games. He picked up some of their language. They taught him tricks with the bow and arrow.

Bill and his father used the wagon mules for rolling logs into place on the walls of their new house. Bill liked the mules. But he wished he had a pony.

He told one of the Indian boys, a lad named Long Bow, about this wish. Long Bow was about Bill's age, and they had taken a liking to each other. The next day, Long Bow came riding up on his own black-and-white paint horse. He was leading a pony. Bill looked at that pony and knew right away he had to have it.

The pony was hard-fleshed, trim-legged. His neck was delicately curved, and his head small. His body was short. That meant power. His hips were curved like a greyhound's. That meant speed.

*Bill looked at that pony and knew right away
he had to have it*

But what Bill liked most about him were his unusual markings. The pony was white, freckled over with black spots. He surely was an eye-catcher—a regular show horse.

Bill was notching the end of a log when the Indian boy rode up. He leaned on the end of his axe and eyed the pony.

"Hiyu, Long Bow," Bill said.

"Haugh," the Indian boy responded.

"That's quite a fancy pony you've got there."

Long Bow could speak a little English. "Like him?" he asked.

"You bet. Want to trade?"

"Him—him—" Long Bow made signs that the horse might buck. "You bust him?"

"Sure," Bill answered with great confidence. He'd never even seen a real bucking horse.

Long Bow said, "No trade. Me give-um." His black eyes were shining with pleasure.

Bill's father had come up. "What does the Indian want?" he asked.

"He wants to give me the spotted pony," Bill said excitedly. "Can I have him, Father? Can I?"

[44]

"Hmm. You sure make friends fast, boy— Is the horse broken, Long Bow?"

The Indian shook his head.

"I can break him, Father. I know I can," Bill boasted.

His father looked at him gravely. Then his eyes began to twinkle.

"Well, boy, I guess you got your heart set on it. But you got to break him yourself. And in your spare time, too. Maybe you'll learn something. Take him out where the ground's soft when you try."

"Thanks, Father!"

"Your mother'd skin me alive if she knew about this," Mr. Cody remarked.

"Thanks! Thanks a heap," Bill said. "Wait, Long Bow."

He tied the pony to a willow tree. Then, after a whispered talk with his father, Bill climbed into the wagon. He came out with a keen, bone-handled bowie knife in a leather sheath. He held out the knife to Long Bow.

The Kickapoo boy looked at it longingly, but didn't reach for it.

"No trade," he said. "Me give-um pony."

[45]

"That's right," Bill answered. "No trade. Me give-um knife."

Long Bow looked Bill in the eye for a minute. Then he reached slowly for the knife. He took it out of the sheath and rubbed his finger over the keen blade. Then he put it into the sheath again and tucked it in the waistband of his leggings.

"Haugh," he said again. He raised his hand and rode off.

Bill immediately named the pony Prince.

The next day was Sunday. Isaac and Bill were glad to knock off for a day of rest after a hard week's work. But the chopping and lifting had begun to harden Bill's muscles. He washed his clothes in the creek after breakfast. Then he decided to start training Prince.

"Better not try to ride him right off," his father said. "Let him get used to you first."

They had no saddle along, but the Indian boy had left the hackamore and tie-rope. Bill led the horse down to the creek to drink. He had already given him his breakfast. The pony went along readily. While he was drinking, the

boy laid his hand lightly on the pony's withers.
Prince trembled a little and switched his tail.
But he didn't shy off.

Back in camp Bill took a piece of rope to use
for reins and tied it to the hackamore. With
the pony tied to the tree, he eased a folded
blanket onto his back. Prince scrounged down.

"Easy now, pony. Easy, Prince," Bill spoke
to him in a soothing voice.

Prince relaxed a bit. Bill patted his neck.

"That's it," Bill told him. "No one is going
to hurt you."

[47]

The boy took the blanket off and put it back on. Prince didn't seem to mind now. So Bill got a cloth surcingle. He laid it gently over the blanket.

"Well, I guess you're a good horse after all," he said.

Very quietly he reached under Prince's belly. He buckled the surcingle and slowly drew it tight. Though Prince tensed a bit, he didn't offer to buck, kick, or bite. He certainly wasn't bad-tempered.

Bill left the pony to get used to the feel of the cinched blanket. He went over to his father, who was sitting against one of the wagon wheels, reading the Bible.

"He must have been ridden," Bill said. "I'm going to try him."

"All right. But be careful," Isaac told him.

Bill untied the pony. He fastened the tie-rope around his neck. Holding the rope reins, he put his left hand on Prince's withers. The horse stood still. Bill put his right hand on his back. Still the horse didn't move.

Bill gave a little jump and straightened his

[48]

elbows. The horse started to walk off. Bill threw his right leg across, and away they went up the valley.

After a while Bill dared to touch Prince's ribs with his heels. The pony broke easily into a trot. Of his own accord he raised this to a lope. Soon he was going at a run. Bill didn't know it, but Prince was headed for home—for the Kickapoo village.

Bill could ride at any ordinary gait without trouble. Well pleased, he let out a war whoop. The pony ran faster. Presently Bill decided they'd gone far enough and he'd better head back to camp.

He tightened up on the reins and tried to turn the horse to the left. Prince just stuck his nose out and ran faster. Bill took a good grip on the reins. He held his elbows close to his sides and leaned back hard.

But Prince decided to argue the point. He was headed for home. No young clothespin of Bill's weight was going to stop him. The harder Bill pulled, the more annoyed the pony became.

[49]

Presently he gave a kick and a wiggle. Bill stuck. The pony stopped running and started to "crow-hop." Bill's head began to flop. His backbone felt as though someone were pounding him on both ends with a sledgehammer.

But he wouldn't quit. So right then Prince decided it was time to teach his rider a lesson. He jumped high and twisted like a snake. He left the boy hanging in the air. And off went Prince, kicking and squealing like a pig at a country fair.

CHAPTER SIX

A Stranger Helps Out

LUCKILY the ground was soft. Bill took up some of the shock of landing by rolling on his back. He flipped over in a somersault and came up running. Prince was well up the divide that led out of the valley.

Bill started off at a trot up the slope. When he reached the top he was winded. He sat down to rest. Stretched out before him lay the prairie. Bright green under the Sunday sun, it spread away in long waves like a calm sea.

Small as insects, a band of antelope filed over a ridgetop. The group of scattered dots in the distance looked like buffalo. And a mile away below, the spotted pony was going at a steady lope.

"Somewhere in this mess of hills," Bill thought, "is the Kickapoo village. It means home to Prince. That must be where he's going."

The boy wondered what to do.

"I sure can't catch him. But maybe I can keep him in sight—or track him home."

Bill made up his mind.

"Father'll wonder where I am. But I can't help it. I'm not going to lose Prince."

He got up and started down the slope. The springy turf made walking easy, and he swung along at a good pace. Prince had slowed to a walk at the foot of the next rise. He kept snatching mouthfuls of the juicy new grass.

Prince was about halfway up when a rider came in sight over the green crest of the ridge ahead. Behind him shouldered a string of loaded pack horses. Three other riders were herding the pack train.

The pony pricked up his ears, and watched them. One of the pack horses whinnied. They drew near the spotted pony. The lead rider untied his rope from the fork of his saddle. Prince laid back his ears and started off at a run.

The rider shook out a small loop. Forty feet of rawhide sang out. The loop settled just behind the runaway's ears. The sudden jerk turned him clear around. A surprised look on his face, he stood with forefeet planted, facing his captor.

The roper paid no attention to the horse. He turned down the slope toward Bill. Prince followed meekly behind. He'd learned, the hard way, not to fight a rope.

Bill ran as fast as he could to meet them. The man was young and limber. He wore fringed buckskin shirt and leggings. There were colored beads across the chest of the shirt. A wolfskin cap was pushed back from his sweaty forehead. The cap had a double tail so long it lay across his shoulder.

The rider looked down on the boy and laughed deep in his chest. He saw streaks of grass-green and dirt on Bill's clothes.

"You don't mean to say this measly little fleabitten pony set you afoot on your hands?" he teased.

[53]

Bill looked up at the tanned face and laughed back.

"He sure did. And I'm glad you caught him!"

"If I hadn't, you'd have had to trail him plumb to California."

The pack horses had come up and gone to grazing. The three men who were herding them had long beards. Their hair flowed over their shoulders. They slouched in their saddles and waited.

Bill said, "It's the first time I've ridden him. He's an Indian pony, and he wanted to go home."

"I'd give it just as a horseback opinion." the man said, "that this speckled beauty is plumb salty. Want me to ride some of the rough off him?"

Bill swallowed. "All right," he answered.

The rider slipped the loop from Prince's head, while Bill held the pony. Then he took the reins from Bill and swung aboard.

One of the bearded trappers had moved up behind Bill. He said, "Watch this, son. If that cayuse has got any ginger, you're going to see a ride."

The spotted pony didn't attempt to buck. The rider touched him with his big-roweled spurs. He guided him in the direction Bill had come from.

Prince moved off sulkily. He still wanted to go home. He kept trying to turn back.

The trapper raised his voice. "Turn him a-loose, Horace! You're leavin' a trail like a snake with a broken back. Turn him a-loose and let him ramble."

Horace looked back and smiled. He rolled his blunt spurs along the pony's ribs.

Prince exploded. He jumped straight up in the air. He bunched his feet and came down hard, stiff-legged. Horace dug in his spurs.

Prince squealed and reached for the sun with his forefeet. He tried to kick a chunk out of a cloud with his hind feet.

Bill was so tense he couldn't swallow.

"Ya-hoo-o-o!" yelled a trapper. "Ain't that pony a bunch of firecrackers?"

Prince made another leap. He rolled over in the air till the sun flashed on his sweating belly. He came down and reared on his hind legs.

Horace touched him again with his spurs. The pony went into a series of racking bucks.

But soon he began to tire. Sweat was pouring off his ribs in rivulets. He broke into a run, still trying to circle toward the Indian camp. The rider spurred him again and pulled his head around. At last Prince straightened out in the direction he was supposed to go.

The stranger turned him back, stepped off, and handed the reins to Bill.

"Reckon he'll behave now," he said.

"Boy, do I wish I could ride like that!" Bill exclaimed.

"Might be I'd teach you," the man said.

[57]

The pony rolled his belly toward the sun

"The whole secret of riding a bucker, son, is balance. Don't tighten up. You'll only get a pounding if you try to hang on by main force."

"I'll sure remember that," Bill said.

"Do you know a good place to camp?" the man asked.

"Come back and camp with us on Salt Creek," Bill suggested. "My father'll want to thank you for catching the pony."

"Sounds like a good idea," the rider said.

They got back on their horses and headed for camp.

As they went they talked. It turned out that the men had been to California hunting for gold. They hadn't had much luck. They had spent the winter trapping. The pack horses were loaded with their winter's catch of furs.

The rider said, "I'm looking for a man named Elijah Cody. He's supposed to be a trader 'round here somewhere. You wouldn't have heard of him, would you?"

"Why, yes," Bill said. "He's my uncle. He lives in Weston."

"Well now! Is that a fact?" the man said.

"He's my uncle too. My name's Horace Billings."

"Then we're cousins," Bill said excitedly. "I'm Bill Cody."

"I'll be switched! You're Isaac's boy. I've heard of you."

Horace turned in the saddle. "Hey, fellers," he shouted to the men behind. "This lad is my cousin, Bill Cody."

When they reached camp, Bill's father was pacing up and down.

"You sure took a long ride, boy," he said. "I was about to get on a mule and hunt you up."

"Prince wanted to go back to his Indian home," Bill explained. "When I tried to stop him, he bucked me off. Father, this is my cousin. He roped Prince, and rode him for me. He's looking for Uncle Elijah."

"Well, you happened along just in time," Isaac said, shaking hands. "Cousin, eh? You must be the long-lost Horace Billings."

"That's me. Glad to know you. I heard Uncle Lije was in the trading business. I thought he might buy my winter's fur catch."

"I reckon he would, at that."

Horace introduced the other men.

"Well, climb off and eat," Isaac told them. "On Sunday we cook up enough to last awhile. So there's plenty."

They all ate heartily. When they had finished, Isaac Cody told them that some soldiers had stopped in while Bill was away.

"They came from the fort," he said. "Someone stampeded a big bunch of their horses and drove them off. And they were out looking for them. They said the Government would pay ten dollars a horse to anyone who'd find them and bring them back."

"That looks like a good job for us," Horace said to his companions. "We'll get rid of these furs and then go horse hunting."

Bill's eyes sparkled. "Father, can I go too?" he asked.

"I don't know, Bill," his father replied. "I don't reckon Horace would want you in the way. He'd have enough to do without looking after you."

"I'd like to have him go," Horace said.

[*61*]

"That fast pony of his would be good to have along. We'll make a regular roundup horse out of him. Yep! I'd like to take them both."

"Well, we'll think about it," Isaac Cody said.

And Bill would think about it, too. He lay awake a long time that night, imagining himself riding the range on Prince with his plainsman cousin.

CHAPTER SEVEN

The Kickapoo Village

HORACE and his bearded partners left early next morning for Elijah Cody's trading post. Days passed. Bill began to wonder if his cousin was really coming back. Each day seemed longer than the last.

His father noticed his anxiety.

"Don't get all in a lather, son," he said. "He'll come or he won't come. Pushing on the bit won't bring him any quicker."

Then one evening Bill was kneeling by the campfire. A many-colored sunset was burning over the hill behind him. He was leaning over the black three-legged Dutch oven, skillfully kneading biscuit dough with the tips of his fingers.

When the thick biscuits were carefully laid around the bottom of the oven, he looked up. In front of him the road climbed out of the valley toward Leavenworth. It went out of sight over a rounded hilltop that stood out clearly in the evening light.

As Bill looked, a rider rose against the tinted sky. Behind him walked a loaded pack horse. They came ambling slowly down the slope. Bill watched a minute to make sure. Then he jumped up with a whoop.

"Father!" he yelled. "It's Horace! He's come back!"

Forgetting all about his biscuits, Bill ran out to meet his plainsman cousin.

Chuckling, his father smoothed out a level bed of coals at the edge of the fire. He set the Dutch oven on it. He put the heavy, cast-iron cover over the oven. Then, with a slab of bark, he shoveled red coals on top. In ten minutes the biscuits would be a rich, golden brown.

With Bill walking at his stirrup, Horace Billings rode into camp.

"We're glad to see you back," Isaac said.

"The boy was about to come untied and hit your trail."

"He needn't have worried," Horace said. "I need him on that horse hunt. My partners decided not to go."

Horace was unsaddling as he talked. He cast off the squaw hitch from his pack horse. He coiled his pack rope. Then he pulled the buffalo-hide cover from the sawbuck pack saddle.

Bill's eyes bugged out at what he saw tied on top. A real stock saddle with a horn for roping.

"Do you reckon that there rig'll fit the spotted pony?" Horace asked.

"You bet!" was all Bill could think of to say.

Isaac was busy about the fire, but watching all the same. Horace went to his pack bag. He fished out a bridle, bit and spurs, and passed them to Bill.

Bill took them, still bug-eyed and speechless.

Horace went back to his pack and came out with a brand-new rawhide rope.

"That's the outfit," he said as he passed it to

Bill. "You're all set now to go to work, boy."

"I don't know's we ought to accept all that," Bill's father said. "That's an awful lot of plunder."

"Don't worry," Horace told him. "The boy'll earn it."

Bill was so busy admiring his new outfit, he'd forgotten all about supper.

Horace's horses took a good roll and headed for the creek. Isaac started dishing out stew and biscuits.

After supper they sat in the warm glow of the campfire while Horace told tales of his adventures in the Far West. Then they rolled up in their beds and fell asleep to the music of the creek.

Next morning Bill got a good look at his new saddle. It was a fancy black one with silver disks that flashed in the sun. Steer heads were carved in the leather.

The bridle had silver bit chains. The Mexican spurs had rowels three inches across.

After breakfast Bill put the new rig on Prince and swung cockily into the saddle.

The dark-haired boy in his homespun pants

and hickory shirt sat up straight. The black saddle and bridle stood out against the white of the pony. Bill touched Prince's ribs gently with the side of the blunt spurs. Prince stepped out quietly.

"Now, ain't that a pretty sight!" Horace said.

"It sure is," Isaac agreed. "I guess that pony's so proud of his new outfit, he forgot to buck."

Bill lifted Prince to a trot. He circled, and then came galloping straight for camp. He let out a war whoop, and pulled up in a shower of gravel.

Prince turned his head and looked up at the boy as though to say, "Hey! What's going on?"

"Are you practicin' up for a circus?" Horace asked.

"That's what!" Bill answered, laughing.

"I reckon they'd hire you two at that," Horace said.

Horace stayed around camp for a few days helping Bill train the pony, and giving the boy kindergarten lessons in roping.

At last one morning they set out on their

first horse hunt. Horace was astride a rangy mustard-colored cow horse. Bill rode Prince. They headed toward Leavenworth. At the top of the hill leading out of the valley, they looked around.

To the north was mostly open prairie. About four miles across it, wooded hills rose again. Beyond these hills flowed Plum Creek. It met Salt Creek a few miles to the east. Together they flowed into the great Missouri.

Somewhere in that great rolling pasture was the reservation of the Kickapoo Indians.

As Horace looked over the green country-side, a plan of action came to him.

"I'll bet those horses are in the triangle between the two creeks. Most likely they've joined a bunch of wild horses. We'll start a little west of here, and comb the country, headed east. Any horses we find we'll drive toward the fork of the creeks."

They ranged far and wide over the valley. But by noon they had found no horses.

They had been getting hungry, and were thinking about stopping for lunch. Suddenly they came out on the flat top of a green hill. There, spread out in a great semicircle, was the Kickapoo village.

All the tall wigwams faced the east. Below them at the foot of the hill, a herd of ponies grazed. They were guarded by Indian boys.

Dogs barked as Bill and Horace approached. At the noise, one Indian left the herd and came galloping toward them on his pony.

As they came near, Bill saw it was Long Bow. He pulled up as the horse hunters raised their arms, palms forward, in the sign of greeting.

Horace began to rub his stomach and point to his mouth.

"Come," Long Bow said, and led the way into the village.

The flaps of the wigwams were tied back. Bill could look inside as they passed. All around the inside edge of each tent was a bed of corn husks, six inches deep. The centers were swept clean with twig brooms. Inside

some tents, girls were grinding corn and edible roots. Inside other tents, other girls were sewing skins together with cactus fiber thread and bone needles. Small, naked children were playing in the open place made by the half-circle of tents.

The elders gathered round. When they learned that Bill and Horace were friends of Long Bow, they made them welcome.

The Indian boy's mother dished out bowls of hot stew. It was made of dried venison cut in small pieces, and cooked with several kinds of

roots and hominy. Bill thought he could learn to like it, once he got used to the lack of salt.

They also had flat corncakes cooked in the hot ashes of the open fire. The Indian children washed off the ashes in cold water. Then they

*"Come," Long Bow said, and led the way
into the village*

spread wild honey on the corncakes. Bill found the cakes were delicious.

After dinner the men sat around the fire and passed the peace pipe. Horace gave the Indians some of his own tobacco which pleased them.

Bill and Long Bow hid inside one of the wigwams and listened. Children were not allowed at grown-up councils.

Bill peered out and saw Horace talking in sign language. Horace made the Indians understand that he wanted to know where the cavalry horses were.

Perhaps some of these Indians had driven the horses away from the fort. Anyway, none of them gave him any information. They only grunted and shook their heads.

Bill and Long Bow were lying on the cornhusk bed at the edge of the wigwam. They could look and listen through the open flap.

Long Bow whispered, "Me know where horses. Me show you. You and friend go north. Me catch up."

Bill whispered, "Thanks, Long Bow."

CHAPTER EIGHT

The Roundup

Bill and Horace left the Indian village as soon as they could. They were only a mile away when a pounding of hoofs sounded behind them. Long Bow rode up. He pointed to the high line of hills off to the north.

"Army horses up there," he said.

"That's a likely place for them," Horace agreed.

"Let's go," Bill yelled.

He touched heel to Prince and flew across the valley. Long Bow went flying after him on the broad-striped paint horse, but he couldn't keep up.

Bill circled and came back. He came to a

sliding stop in front of his cousin. Long Bow did the same.

Horace was angry. He drew down his eyebrows and said sternly, "I don't want any more of that. Save your horses for the work."

They rode up a high hill which was thickly wooded. As they reached the upper edge of the trees, a shrill whistle suddenly sounded above them.

The bare dome of the hill was a rich pasture of curly buffalo grass. On top, peering toward them, stood the wildest-looking creature Bill had ever seen.

It was a small, shaggy brown pony. His mane came to his knees. His thick forelock almost hid his eyes.

"Wild horse," Long Bow said.

"He's a sentinel, standing guard," Horace added. "He must have some mares around."

As he spoke, the wild sentinel's band came up behind him. There were about thirty mares and a few colts. Heads lifted, they came slowly forward. About three hundred yards away they stopped. The three riders were sitting quietly at the edge of the woods. Prince nickered.

At some unseen signal the band stood still while the shaggy leader started down the slope.

He trotted carefully along. His head swung from side to side, searching the wind for scent. Sometimes he put his nose to the ground like a hound dog on trail.

Bill held his breath. "Why don't they run?" he asked. "Why is he coming toward us?"

"He don't know what we are," Horace explained. "He heard us. He knows there's a horse around. That's all. Now he's trying to

smell us out. A horse's ears are mighty keen. His nose is, too. But his eyes ain't so good."

"Wind against him," Long Bow said.

"That's right," Horace agreed. "If he don't catch man scent soon, he's liable to come charging in with his teeth bared, ready to take a chunk out of something."

Horace yelled. The wild horse turned so fast he seemed to go inside out. He whistled as he turned, and went streaking back up the hill.

[77]

Horace spurred his horse after him. Long Bow and Bill followed.

The band of wild horses disappeared over the hilltop. Halfway up, Bill and Prince went by Horace like a shot.

"Don't get too far ahead of us," Horace shouted.

The wild ones had a downhill start. When Bill reached the top of the hill, they had disappeared in the trees.

Bill stopped. Horace and Long Bow pulled up beside him. They could hear the wild ones crashing through the timber below.

Beyond the foot of the hill was open prairie again. Out there another bunch of horses was grazing.

"Army horses," Long Bow said.

"You must be right," Horace agreed after watching a moment. "If they were wild they'd have a leader herding them."

"Me know," Long Bow said. "Army horses stay near wild horses. No come too close."

"You're right, they won't," Horace said. "That little wild leader would sure bite a piece

[*78*]

out of any tame horse that came near his mares. But horses like company. So the army horses stick as close as the boss of the wild bunch will let them."

Just at this point the wild bunch came out of the trees. The leader saw the army horses. He screamed with rage. He stretched out his neck and made for them, his teeth showing.

The army horses lifted their heads from the grass. They took one look and went streaming away up the valley, with the wild bunch hot on their high-held tails.

"Let's go, boys," Horace ordered. "Keep spread out. Let them go unless they try to turn back. Then stop them!"

Horace and Bill and Long Bow weaved back and forth across the narrowing plain to stop a break back. The army horses were the first to come to the frothing fork where Salt and Plum Creeks plunged together. The water was high from melting snow and spring rains.

They saw it was too fast and deep to swim, and started to turn back. But they ran right into the wild bunch.

As the stallion came by, he made a fast toss

The shaggy little stallion screamed and tore a piece of flesh from one of the army horses. He turned and began to kick. His hard hoofs sounded like the crack of bat on ball as he smacked his enemies' ribs.

The army horses crowded along the shore past the wild ones, out of reach.

The three riders sat their saddles and waited tensely.

Horace shouted, "That little devil will surely try to get past us now. If we can rope him, maybe we can hold the rest."

He was getting his rope ready as he spoke. He shook out a loop—and none too soon. The fiery little horse turned from the river and, head lowered, charged straight back. His mares came with him.

Horace kicked up his horse, and as the stallion came by, he made a fast toss. But the rat-quick pony dodged. A mare came along, stepped in the loop and went down.

The wild one was off again. Bill raced after him. The little stallion's hoofs fairly twinkled with speed. His long mane and tail streamed in the breeze.

[*81*]

But Prince went thundering after him. Bill untied the saddle strings that held his rope. He built a loop the way Horace had taught him.

Prince had almost caught up with the stallion. Bill twirled his loop twice, took careful aim, and let go.

The loop settled fairly around the stallion's brown neck. Bill quickly twisted his rope around the saddle horn. He brought Prince back on his haunches.

The little wild horse's tongue came out as the rope brought him to a choking stop.

He swung around, with fire in his eye, and charged straight at Prince.

But Horace, with Long Bow's help, had untangled his rope from the mare. The two rode up to Bill at a run. Skillfully, Horace threw a loop under the flashing front hoofs. His rangy mount sat back on his haunches. The stallion went on his nose.

Long Bow jumped off his horse and sat on the wild one's head. Then Horace hog-tied three feet and the little wild horse lay still.

[*82*]

"I reckon you'll be good for a spell now," Horace told him as he coiled his rope. "Now we've got you where we want you, we can mix your mares and colts in with the army horses."

He stood up. "Who's that coming?"

Bill looked up. Coming across the plain from the west was a buckboard drawn by a handsome team of mules.

"Don't know," Bill said.

Long Bow gave a quick glance. "Russell," he said.

But by now the herd was starting to move off. The three riders rounded them up, and drove them back to the river's fork.

As they finished, the man in the buckboard came along and stopped his team. He was a tall man with a long beard and grave eyes. He looked at Bill and smiled.

"What's your name, lad?" he asked.

"Bill Cody."

"Is that so? I know your father. A good man. Well, son, anyone who can ride and rope the way you can at your age is going to do all right. My name's Russell. If you ever want a job, just look me up in Leavenworth."

"Thanks, Mr. Russell," Bill said. He was flabbergasted by the praise from this famous man.

"Are you the Russell that runs the big freighting company at Leavenworth?" Horace asked.

"That's me," the bearded man replied. "Do you want to sell those mustangs?"

"Sure thing," Horace answered.

"I can use them. Just drive them into our corral at Leavenworth. You can sort out the army horses when you get there."

Mr. Russell picked up the reins and rattled off toward the fort.

"Looks like the old man's taken a shine to you, Bill," Horace said. "Maybe there'll be a good chance for you with his outfit someday."

The three horse hunters headed the big band of horses toward the fort.

Then Horace went back to the little wild leader. He knew that the little stallion would try to fight for his mares if he turned him loose. So he took a wide piece of rawhide with a slit in each end, and slipped a front hoof through each slit.

Then he unwrapped his "piggin" string from the pony's ankles. The little beast strug-

[85]

gled to his feet. He could graze, but he could not walk fast. Later they'd come back and take off the hobble and let him go.

This was only the first of several horse hunts. Billy learned to use a rope well before they were through. He had lots of practice riding with Horace, and tracking.

At last, however, all the horses were captured and Horace left to seek other adventures. Bill would have liked to go with him, but his father needed him to help on the farm.

CHAPTER NINE

Bloody Kansas

ISAAC CODY pulled the high-piled hayrack up beside the new log wagon shed. Skillfully turning the four mules, he began to back the hayrack under the shed.

Bill slid off the top of the load. As soon as the wagon stopped, he hustled to unhook the mules. He was starving.

All day he and his father had been getting in the young crop of hay. Tomorrow they were to start delivering it to Fort Leavenworth.

It was a late June evening, over a year after the horse hunt. A full moon was growing yellow in the east. The sweet smell of fresh-cut hay filled the air.

Bill had hayseed down his neck and back, clear to his belt. His face was streaked with dusty sweat. He watered and fed the mules as fast as he could, and then he raced for the creek. He plunged into the cool water and washed off the day's grime.

The cabin had been finished early in the spring, and Bill's mother and sisters had come from Weston to join Mr. Cody and Bill. As he swam, Bill thought of the good supper his mother had ready for them.

"Willie," it was Lydia calling, "Willie, get out of that creek! If you're late for supper you won't get any."

"That's what you think!" Bill yelled back.

But tonight he didn't have to be called twice. His stomach felt like an empty cave. He slipped on his pants and rushed into the house, streaming water.

His sisters screamed at him as he left muddy footprints on their white, scrubbed floor. But Bill didn't answer. He went into his own room to put on clean clothes.

When he came out, supper was steaming on

[*88*]

the table. His father looked gravely at him as he slid into his chair and bowed his head. Isaac asked the blessing. Bill could hardly wait for him to get through before he began to stuff corn bread into his mouth with one hand, and kidney beans with the other.

"Watch your manners, Bill," Lydia scolded.

"You watch yours!" Bill shot back.

"Now, stop it, children," their mother said. "I'll do the manners watching."

Bill laughed. He'd have been lonesome without any sisters to fight with. It was all in fun.

He loved this fine log house he had helped to build. He had his own room, and his sisters had theirs, and his father and mother had theirs. The rest was all one big living room, kitchen, and dining room. It had a great fireplace at one end.

When Bill and his father had finished building the house, they had built a stable and wagon shed. They had also put up a small building with shelves and a counter in it for a trading post. Since Mr. Cody was too busy to

[*89*]

give much time to trading, this building was not as big as Riveley's trading post near Fort Leavenworth.

Now Bill was stowing away an enormous supper, thinking how well he liked this life. He was glad that he and his father were going to take hay to Fort Leavenworth the next day. They would probably stop at the office of the huge freighting company. Then Bill would see his friend Mr. Russell.

The boy's thoughts were interrupted by his mother's voice. "What's on your mind, Isaac?" she asked Bill's father. "Why are you so quiet tonight?"

"This valley is sure getting full of people," Isaac said.

"And don't you like that?"

"A family with a lot of slaves have taken some land about a mile from here. They aim to use slaves to farm it."

"Why let it worry you, Isaac?" asked Mrs. Cody. "The people in Kansas voted to allow slaveowners to settle here."

"Ann, you know very well how that hap-

[*90*]

pened!" Bill's father exclaimed. "Several thousand men rode across from Missouri and voted, even though they had no right to. Then they rode back again. They even brought guns and a cannon along, so that no one could stop them from voting."

"There's nothing you can do about it, Isaac," said Mrs. Cody. "Quit fretting."

"I can't, Ann. This is supposed to be a democracy. But if men can back up their votes with guns and cannon, we don't have democracy."

Bill had been listening intently. Suddenly, without thinking, he said, "We got to fight, Ma. We got to fight! We can't let them run over us."

"What do you know about it, smarty?" Lydia put in.

"Well, let's not fight among ourselves, anyway," their mother said. Her voice was tired when she added, "There's been too much fighting. Why can't people live together in peace?"

Mr. Cody stood up. "Come on, Bill," he

[*91*]

Next morning, Bill and his father left early
for Leavenworth

said. "We've both finished eating and it's time we got our chores done."

Next morning, Bill and his father left early for Leavenworth. It took six mules to haul their load of hay over the big hill.

Fort Leavenworth had been built twenty years before Bill was born, to protect the people who traveled on the Santa Fe Trail. It had grown to be the supply depot for every army fort in the West, clear to California.

Bill and his father drove past the guard-house, and left the hay at the old log stables on the south side of the big parade ground.

When the hay had been delivered, they set out for the town of Leavenworth. Bill persuaded his father to let him drive. The six mules were a handful for him. But he managed them well.

At the southeast side of the parade ground were two old log barracks. From the barracks an old stone wall ran to a blockhouse—the only defense against the Indians in the early days. Isaac told Bill to turn the mules off there, and they headed south for the new town.

"This place is sure growing fast," Bill said.

"I've never seen anything like it," his father agreed. "There were eight hundred folks in Kansas when we came, and eight thousand last fall. Don't know how many now. Russell's is growing, too. Look at that new warehouse."

Russell, Majors and Waddell was the biggest freighting company in the West. The owners had nearly 8,000 men working for them. They had over 6,000 big covered freight wagons and 75,000 oxen. They owned tens of thousands of Texas longhorns which they sold to the army for meat.

Their great freight outfits fingered out into the West in every direction. With its stables, corrals, blacksmith shops, warehouses, and offices, their place was like a little city.

Bill and his father were going to stop for supplies at one of the warehouses. When they came in sight of it, Bill spied his friend Russell on the loading platform.

The boy clucked to the mules till they were going at a smart trot. At the warehouse he pulled up with a flourish. Mr. Russell squinted at him with a twinkle in his eye. He turned to Bill's father.

"I see you've got a long-line mule skinner in the family, Mr. Cody," he said.

"If he doesn't slow down in the middle of town," Isaac answered, "I'll skin *him*."

"For a nine-year-old he's doing all right," Mr. Russell said.

The two men laughed and went inside while Bill held the mules. In a few minutes two clerks brought the supplies and loaded them in the wagon. Then Isaac came out again, and he and Bill headed home.

When they came near Riveley's trading post they saw a crowd of men. One was standing on a dry goods box, waving his arms.

"I wonder what's going on?" Bill said.

"Looks like that fellow is making a speech," Isaac answered. "It must be a political meeting."

As they got closer they could hear the speaker's voice. But the man jumped down before they were near enough to make out what he was saying.

[*95*]

"Isn't that Charlie Dunn?" Bill asked.

"It is at that," Isaac replied. "Let's stop and speak to him."

He pulled up the empty hayrack at the edge of the crowd, and handed the reins to Bill. Jumping out, he went up to Dunn and shook hands.

"Hello, Charlie. How's your family?" he asked.

"They're all well," Dunn answered.

But before Isaac could go on, Dunn turned to the crowd. "Here's someone we ought to hear from, men," he said. "Mr. Cody's a fine speaker. He could be a lot of help to us."

Isaac knew some of the men, for they were his neighbors.

"Yes, let's hear from you, Cody," one of them said. "You've been around here longer than most of us. And we don't know where you stand on this slavery question."

The crowd seemed friendly. Bill's father knew he would have to let people know what side he was on sooner or later. Perhaps now was a good time.

He stepped up on the dry goods box. Bill watched him anxiously. The crowd grew quiet, and Isaac began to speak.

"Gentlemen," he said, "you have called upon me for a speech. Perhaps my ideas will not be the same as yours. The question before us today is: Shall slaveowners be allowed to live in Kansas? Shall Kansas become a slave state?

"Friends, I am, and always have been, opposed to slavery. It is bad both for the slave and for the slaveholder. I pledge you my word that I shall lay down my life, if need be, to keep Kansas a free state."

Hoots and hisses rose from the crowd at this statement. Bill grew tense on the wagon seat as he listened. The mules sensed his fear, and began to prance. The boy climbed down from the wagon. He took the round iron hitching weight from the wagon, and snapped it to a bit ring.

When the mules were fastened, he went over to the crowd. The shouts were getting louder:

"Get down from that box, Isaac Cody!"

"Shoot him!"

"Kill him!"

Bill stood in front of the big dry goods box. He listened fearfully as his father went on speaking.

Dunn was standing near him. Bill saw Dunn's face growing red with rage.

"He must have thought Father would take the other side," Bill said to himself.

Suddenly Dunn shouted, "Get down off that box, Cody—before I pull you down!"

Isaac paused, startled, and looked at him. Then he went calmly on with his speech.

Dunn circled the box. He pulled a long bowie knife from his belt. With the swift movement of a cat he jumped up on the platform. The knife flashed in the afternoon sunlight and plunged deep into Isaac's back.

Isaac stumbled from the box. Dunn jumped on the wounded man like a wildcat. But two strong men grabbed him by the arms and pulled him away.

Bill dropped on his knees by his father, who was unconscious. He ripped off his shirt and tore it into strips. Neighbors helped him bind Isaac Cody's wound.

"We'd better get him in the hay wagon. The boy can drive him home," one of the neighbors said.

"I don't think we ought to move him," said another. "I think that knife went into a lung. We'd better put him to bed in Riveley's house till we can get a doctor from the fort."

"What side is Riveley on—slave or free?"

At that moment Riveley himself drove up in a buckboard from Leavenworth. When he heard what had happened, he said, "Get him

[*99*]

inside. No matter what I think of slavery, I don't go for this sort of thing."

Bill helped the men carry his father into the trading post. They laid him carefully on the bed.

Riveley, a tall, bony man, turned to the boy. He put a hand on Bill's shoulder, and said gently, "He'll probably be all right, son. But you better get along home and bring your mother over here. I'll send for the doctor."

Dazed, Bill went out. He tossed the hitching weight into the wagon and climbed into the seat. With a lump in his throat, he put the mules into a fast trot for home.

He was white-faced and his eyes were full of fear. Gripping the reins tightly, he sat up straight. What if his father should die?

CHAPTER TEN

Bill and a Bully

BILL, I want you to go to school!"

"But, Ma, I can't. I've got to earn money."

"We'll make out somehow. You'll earn more in the long run if you go to school."

Bill was driving his mother to Leavenworth in the family carriage. Though his father had recovered from the stabbing, he had never been strong again. In April, two years later, he had died from a cold in his weakened lungs.

Bill drove along for a moment before he answered his mother. Then he said, his voice puzzled, "Look, Mother, I've been making twenty-five dollars a month herding cattle for Mr. Russell. Now he doesn't need me to herd any more, but most likely he can find something else for me to do. I don't see how we can live if I don't earn—"

"Maybe I'll start an inn," Mrs. Cody said. "There's need for one in Salt Creek Valley. With so many people passing through, I'd have more business than I wanted."

"Mother! You're not strong enough."

"You'd be surprised at what I can do," his mother replied.

Bill grunted. In the three years since they had come to Kansas, he had grown up a lot. Especially in the last few months since his father had died. It had been a tough time. The Codys had had to sell everything they could spare. The two mules hitched to the carriage, and one cow, were all the stock they had left.

Bill knew his mother had tuberculosis, though she never mentioned it. He was only eleven years old, but he felt that he wanted to take care of her.

Leavenworth was by this time a thriving city. But Russell, Majors and Waddell were still the biggest thing there. Mr. Russell was the business manager. Alexander Majors was in charge of the herds and wagon trains. He was such a friendly man that nearly everyone called him Uncle Alec. Uncle Alec was a good friend of the Cody family.

Before Mrs. Cody could do any shopping, Bill had to collect his pay for the two months of herding. He tied the mules to the hitchrack outside the R. M. & W. office, and he and his mother went in.

A bookkeeper was sitting on a long-legged stool behind a high, sloping desk.

"Morning, Mrs. Cody," he said, getting up. "Hello, Bill. I see you got the trail dust out of your hair. You're all slicked up like Sunday. I reckon you want your pay."

"We could use it, if it's ready," Bill said.

"It's all ready. Just sign the book."

He opened a payroll book on the desk, and pointed to a place where Bill should sign.

Bill knew that his mother was watching him. His face reddened. This was the punishment for the days he'd spent riding his pony when he should have been in school. He found his name and made an X beside it.

[*103*]

"Oh, Billy!" his mother exclaimed. "Can't you even sign your name?" Tears flooded her eyes. "Won't you please, please go to school?"

She bit her lip to hold back the tears, but they streamed down her cheeks. At this point, Uncle Alec came into the room.

"Here, here, what's wrong?" he asked.

Mrs. Cody couldn't answer. Bill spoke up.

"Mother wants me to go to school because I can't sign the payroll."

"And you think you have to work. Is that it?" asked Uncle Alec.

"Yes, sir."

"Hmm. Well—" Alec Majors thought for a moment. "Maybe you can do both," he said. Then he shouted, "Hey, William, come out here a minute."

Mr. Russell's tall figure appeared in the door of his office. He glanced at Bill and at Mrs. Cody, who was wiping her eyes.

Uncle Alec said, "This boy has got to work —and he's got to go to school. See how that fits in with what we were just talking about?"

"Why, so it does," Russell said, his face

pleased. "Bill, we need a man to take messages from the office to the wagon trains that have started out on the road. Plenty of things come up after a train leaves that have to be tended to."

"What we need, really," Uncle Alec put in, "is a sort of office boy on horseback. We'll pay you same as you were getting before. And you can do the work outside of school hours."

"How do you like that, Bill?" Russell asked.

Bill Cody was walking on clouds. "Great!" he said. "That's just great!"

Russell went on, "Give him a good horse, Alec. He's a good rider."

"I know," said Mr. Majors. "He can ride like a man. We'll give him the best."

Mr. Russell patted Bill's mother on the shoulder. "Don't worry, Ann," he said. "You've got a good boy here. He's going to leave a scratch on this little round old world."

So Bill went to school. He was behind the other children of his age, but he worked hard to catch up. Most of the children were friendly. But there was one big bully named Gobol,

[*105*]

who made fun of Bill because he couldn't write his own name.

After school each day Bill went to the offices of R. M. & W. to see if there were any messages to be carried. If there were none, he wandered around the corrals and wagon yards. He liked the smell of horses. The sight of the long wagon trains heading for far places stirred his blood.

When he first learned to write his own name, Bill was so pleased that he wanted to write it all the time. He wrote it with the end of a burnt stick on white wagon covers. He carved it on the sides of wagons, on oxbows, on any smooth piece of wood he could find.

One afternoon Bill was writing his name in big letters across the white cover of a freight wagon. The bully, Gobol, came up behind him. He was a head taller than Bill, and beefy.

"I see you learned to write your name at last," he said with a sneering laugh.

Bill paid no attention to him. He went on with his writing.

Gobol said, "You know you can be arrested

for that—marking up people's property?"

Still Bill said nothing.

"If Mr. Russell saw you doing that, you'd catch it," Gobol went on.

William Frederick Cody was a long name. It would take the whole side of the wagon sheet. Bill had been enjoying himself until Gobol came along. He went on tracing the letter with the burnt stick.

Gobol was angry because he couldn't get Bill to talk back or fight. He said, "I'm going to squeal on you."

He walked off. Bill went on with his work. He was worried now, but he wasn't going to stop because of Gobol. In a little while the bully came back. Mr. Russell was with him.

Billy's back was to them. He was just starting the Y in Cody. He'd really done a fine job.

He heard Mr. Russell say, "Why, Gobol, you just told me it was some boy. If you'd said 'Billy Cody' I wouldn't have bothered to come out. You see, Billy works for me, and I don't mind if he practices writing on those nice big white wagon sheets."

"But—but—" Gobol stammered. He couldn't think what to say. His face reddened and he stalked off.

From then on, he was more than ever Bill's enemy.

When he was out of sight and hearing, Mr. Russell put his hand on Bill's shoulder.

"Son," he said, "that charcoal is sure a mess. I guess it's up to you to wash it off. Whatever got into you to do such a thing, anyway?"

"Why—why—I guess—I just learned to write my name—and it seemed like such a good big place. I—I—"

"I understand," Mr. Russell said. "You wanted everyone to know you could do it. It's all right, boy, but don't do it again. Lew Simpson is going to be mad as a hornet when he sees one of his wagon sheets all smudged up."

Lew Simpson was Alec Major's top wagon master, and a friend of Bill's. Bill hoped someday to go out on trail with him.

"I'll scrub it so clean that Lew will never know," Bill promised. He went to work with a pail of water and a brush.

Bill stayed in school all winter. But by the time spring came, his eyes were looking out the window as often as on his books. Meadow larks were singing, the grass was greening. Little red-and-white calves were dotting the landscape. Long trains of settlers were filing by on their way to Oregon.

Bill longed to be outdoors. But, for his mother's sake, he made up his mind that he wasn't going to quit. Already he could read and write and figure with the best of them. So far he'd managed to keep out of a fight with Gobol.

Steve Gobol often tried to start a fight between Duke, his big bull terrier, and Bill's dog, Turk. But Turk was a good-natured animal. He stuck close to Bill and kept out of trouble.

But one day the bull terrier went too far. He sneaked up and bit Turk from behind.

Turk turned and silently flew at his tormentor. Though the white terrier was bred and trained to fight, he was a town dog. He was no match for the trail dog who had tracked wolves and mountain lions.

In no time at all, Turk had his attacker on his back, teeth sunk in his throat. In a minute he would have killed the terrier. He didn't even hear Bill calling him to let go.

Quickly, Bill leaned over Turk. He forced his fingers into the back of the dog's mouth behind his teeth. Turk had to let go or choke. He rolled his eyes back at Bill as his jaws came open.

Bill leaned over Turk to examine his wounds. With no warning Steve Gobol suddenly hit Bill in the jaw. Bill went over sprawling on his back.

Gobol jumped on him before he could get up. By sheer weight and strength he held the lighter boy down. He started to pound Bill's head on a rock.

Bill felt weak and sick. Everything was turning black and fuzzy. He had a bowie knife that Lew Simpson had given him, which he carried in a sheath on his belt. Now, in desperation, he reached for it and jabbed Gobol in the leg.

The bully screamed and jumped up. He held tightly to his leg, but the blood streamed through his fingers. Steve Gobol was thoroughly scared.

"Help!" he yelled. "Help!"

Bill got groggily to his feet. He heard the bellow of an ox and looked down the street. A long ox-drawn wagon train was coming slowly toward him. Those oxen with their heads low and swinging to their work sure looked good to Bill Cody. Even better, the wagon master, who was riding beside the lead wagon, was Lew Simpson.

Bill looked the other way. The schoolmaster was striding toward him. It didn't take Bill two flips of a mule's ear to decide which way to go.

He got his wobbly legs under control, and headed for the wagon train. He dodged under the noses of a pair of snorting oxen, to the opposite side. When he thought the teacher couldn't see him, he slipped over the tail gate of a wagon. Worming his way to the front, he lay down behind the seat.

Bill was sweating and panting. He shut his eyes and put his hands to his throbbing head.

But he felt safe. He felt sure his friend Lew Simpson would take care of him.

The wagon train kept rolling slowly along. Bill wondered why Simpson didn't come back and talk to him. After a while he heard the

rattling of carriage wheels. Then he heard the sound of angry voices.

Bill peeked through the front of the wagon sheet. There in a buggy was Gobol's father. Beside him was the sheriff of the county.

[*112*]

Mr. Gobol was yelling at Lew Simpson. The wagon master lifted his hand as a stop signal.

"Hold it up, boys!" he hollered. The drivers brought their animals to a halt.

Gobol's father was pointing his buggy whip

at Simpson and shouting, "We know that young rascal Bill Cody is in this wagon train. You better produce him—fast."

"If there's any boy hiding in this train, I don't know it. I never saw him get in any

[*113*]

wagon," Simpson said patiently and truthfully. "And," he added, with an edge to his voice, "I'm not going to be held up while you hunt him."

The sheriff said, "This is a pretty serious thing, Lew. You better let us have a look."

"Have you got a warrant to search these wagons, Tom?" Simpson answered.

"No, but I can get one fast enough."

"Don't bother, Tom," Simpson said softly. "If Bill Cody's on this train, he's got a reason for it. No one's going to take him off."

A shiver ran up Bill's back. He knew tough Lew Simpson meant what he said.

CHAPTER ELEVEN

Bill Goes West

THE wagon train wasn't very far from Bill's house when Mr. Russell came riding along in his buckboard. Simpson had found Bill in his hideout and heard his story. He told Mr. Russell what had happened.

"Come on, Billy," Russell said. "We'll have to go talk to your mother."

Bill climbed into the buckboard beside him and they rode on ahead of the wagons. The boy was feeling pretty badly when they drove up to the cabin. He was glad his sisters were at school.

"What happened, Willie? What are you doing here at this time of day?" his mother asked as they came in.

"The boy's in a little trouble," Russell explained. He told Mrs. Cody the whole story.

"Oh, Willie," she said sadly. "How did you manage to get into such a fight?"

"I don't know, Mother," Bill said, with tears in his eyes. "I didn't aim to."

"I don't think he'd better go back till things quiet down," Mr. Russell went on. "Gobol's father and the teacher are good friends. And the teacher's a mean man. I'm afraid he won't treat Bill right now."

"But he must get an education," Mrs. Cody protested.

"He can go back later," Russell said. "I have another plan for him now. Lew Simpson's taken a fancy to the boy. He can use him to drive the extra oxen and horses that go with his wagon train. They're taking supplies and beef to the western army posts. And they should be back by the end of the summer, if they have luck. We'll pay Bill forty dollars a month in gold if you'll let him go."

"Well, I suppose it's the only thing to do," Bill's mother said.

She set food on the table, and while Bill was eating, she put some extra clothes in a sack. By this time, the long wagon train was slowly passing the cabin.

Bill hugged his mother good-by. She held him tight. He got his fancy saddle from the stables, and joined the train. Lew Simpson pointed out a mule for him to ride. He saddled it and swung aboard.

A wagon train drawn by oxen was called a "bull-train." This was a ten-wagon bull-train. Each wagon had a driver called a bullwhacker. It was a tough outfit, but every man knew his job and did it. There wasn't a bullwhacker among them who couldn't knock a fly off an ox's ear with the tip of his twenty-foot whip.

The freight wagons were called Murphy wagons. They were very large and strongly built. Each wagon was covered by two canvas wagon sheets to keep the load dry. Since the wagons had no seats, the bullwhackers had to walk.

In addition to the bullwhackers and the wagon master, there was an extra man who did

*It was a tough outfit, but every man
knew his job and did it*

odd jobs, a night herder, and a cavayard driver. Bill was the "cavvy" driver. He had to keep all the spare oxen and horses together and out of the way of the wagons. It was a hard job.

Besides the ten wagons there was a herd of Texas longhorn beef cattle. They came along well behind the wagon train, because they kicked up such clouds of dust.

Nothing exciting happened to the men until they had traveled nearly a month. They had passed Fort Kearny on the Platte River, and were about three hundred miles from Leavenworth. One day they were climbing a hill when they saw dust blowing over the top. Then they heard a rumble like thunder. Lew Simpson ordered the bullwhackers to get the wagons off the road quickly. He put spurs to his horse and made a run for the top of the hill.

Bill was driving his "cavvy" behind the wagon train, but he could see Simpson on the hilltop waving frantically for the wagons to hurry. Then Bill saw Lew raise his rifle and fire straight ahead. Lew shot several times as

[119]

fast as he could load his gun. Then he turned and came tearing back down the hill at a high lope.

By this time Bill was driving the "cavvy" off the road onto the prairie. When he had them a little distance away, he looked back.

A frightening black mass of buffalo was pouring over the brow of the hill. Straight for the wagons they headed. Nothing could stop them. Behind them came the hunters who had stampeded them. They pulled up their horses at the top of the hill, took off their hats and

mopped their foreheads as they saw the trouble their carelessness had caused.

The oxen became frightened when they saw the black herd roaring toward them. They tried to run and twisted the wagons every which way. They broke wagon tongues and got tangled up in the gear.

The bullwhackers saw at once that there was nothing they could do. They ran for their lives out of the path of the herd.

The buffalo hit the train and went over it like black surf on a beach. Wagons tipped over. Canvas was torn by the stout horns and sharp hoofs.

One huge bull buffalo got his horn caught in a wagon chain. He bellowed, and shook his shaggy head. Finally he broke the chain, but he couldn't get his horn loose. With the ox yoke that was attached to the chain hanging on his head, he charged straight at Billy Cody.

Bill was having a hard time keeping his frightened "cavvy" from stampeding. He knew that if the buffalo ran into them, they'd scatter over the prairie like dry leaves in a windstorm. Bill dragged out his rifle.

He remembered what he'd heard from plainsmen who had killed many buffalo.

"Shoot just behind the shoulder two thirds of the way down and at a downward angle," the plainsmen had said.

By this time the raging bull was almost on him. Bill jumped his horse out of the way, and as the brute went by, he sighted quickly and pulled trigger. The buffalo was dead before he could stop running. Twenty-five yards beyond Bill, he stumbled and plowed his nose into the earth. He toppled over on his side and lay there, with the ox yoke still linked to one horn.

By this time the buffalo herd had passed on and were thundering away over the prairie. The hunters, who were tenderfeet heading East from California, were all apologies.

Lew Simpson was as polite as he could be at such a time. But he knew it would take his men two days to get their wagons and gear mended and get on the trail again.

On the evening of the stampede the men were sitting around the campfire. An old bull-whacker turned to Bill. "Son, you've got to stop shooting buffalo or we'll have to get us another 'cavvy' driver," he said. "We didn't need no buffalo meat today."

Bill laughed. He felt a thrill go through him. These tough old plainsmen would never praise anyone straight out. But the boy knew this was their way of telling him he had done well.

Three days later, the men started out with the wagon train again. They had gone less than forty miles when they ran into their second mess of trouble.

They were camping one noon on the prairie above the Platte River. They had built a fire and made a good hot meal. Up since dawn, full of dinner, and baked by the sun, the men were very sleepy. They crawled under the shade of the wagons for a snooze. Only three men were left to guard the longhorn cattle.

Suddenly, where the herd was grazing, shots rang out. Frightening war whoops sounded above the drumming of hoofs and the bellowing of cattle. The men who were under the wagons grabbed their rifles and peered out.

Yelling painted Indians were chasing off the

herd of cattle and the saddle horses. They were flapping buffalo robes at the animals to frighten them. The herders were nowhere in sight. Perhaps they had been shot from their horses.

As the stampeded animals disappeared into a dip in the prairie, the Indians circled and charged straight for the camp. Bill lay under a wagon and peered out at the naked riders in their war paint and feathers. The Indians came close. Bill gripped his rifle and sighted along the barrel. He didn't feel afraid—just tense and excited. Perhaps this was because no one else was afraid. To the group of plainsmen around him, this was all in the day's work.

"Let 'em have it, boys," Simpson yelled.

The wagoners fired, and the Indians turned and made off. They started a wide circling of the camp. But one painted warrior lay dead on the grass, while his riderless war horse joined the galloping circle.

Simpson said, "We can't stand them off here. Break for the river. We won't have a better chance."

[*125*]

Bill gripped his rifle and sighted along the barrel

The men crawled out from under the wagons. They sprinted for the high bank of the river. The Indians came charging down again.

But before they could do any damage, the men of the wagon train had scrambled into the creek bed. Young and limber, Bill wasn't the last to jump over the rim and go sliding down in a shower of gravel. Using the bank for a breastworks, they fired another volley. Two more redmen fell, and the Indians retreated.

"Where do we go from here?" one of the men asked.

"The only thing we can do," Lew told them, "is to head down the river. It's about fifty miles back to Fort Kearny. There's lots of cover in the riverbed. If we can fight them off till night, we'll make it."

They started downriver, hugging the banks and keeping under cover as much as they could. Soon they saw clouds of smoke coming up from where the camp had been. The Indians were burning the wagons.

"Hope they're more interested in plunder than scalps," one of the men said.

[*127*]

Lew answered, "We can't take any chances. If I know Injuns, they'll try for scalps. It's up to us to make it tough for them."

The men kept a close watch on the bank. Whenever an Indian showed himself, someone took a shot at him.

It was growing dark, and they hadn't seen an Indian for some time. They hoped the raiders had given up the chase. Billy Cody, though big and strong for his eleven years, was getting tired. Without noticing it, he fell behind the rest of the party.

Suddenly the boy saw a bronzed warrior standing on a bluff above the river. The Indian didn't see him, but he was aiming his gun toward Bill's partners farther down the stream. Bill's heart turned over and seemed to stick in his throat. Almost without thinking, he brought his rifle to his shoulder and fired. The Indian tumbled off the bank into the river bed.

Bill was surprised. He was scared, too. He was afraid the whole band of Indians would be down on them now. While he was standing there wondering what to do next, his friends, who had heard the shot, came running back.

"Who fired that shot?" Lew Simpson asked quietly.

"I did," Bill answered.

"Yes," another man said, who had almost

stumbled over the Indian's body, "and little Billy has killed an Indian stone dead!"

As he spoke, gunfire broke from the bank. The men dropped behind rocks and bushes and shot back. Soon it was so dark that the Indians stopped firing. Most tribes are afraid to

[*129*]

fight after dark. They believe that the spirit of a man who is killed at night cannot go to the happy hunting grounds.

The wagoners sneaked off one by one down the river. It was dawn before the weary outfit reached Fort Kearny.

Lew Simpson put his hand on Bill Cody's shoulder as he told their tale. "Boys," he said at the end, "Billy's downed his first Injun. And he couldn't have done a better job of it, if he'd been a thirty-year scout."

Simpson and some of the others went back with a detachment of troops from the fort. They found the three herders scalped, and the remains of the looted wagons. But they never did catch the red raiders.

CHAPTER TWELVE

Riding the Pony Express

BILL CODY slammed his axe into the chopping block. "Ouch!" he cried. He fingered the red welt on his cheek where a hunk of stovewood had hit him. He wiped the dust out of his eyes, and went back to his wood splitting.

A cold March wind was cutting across the top of Cody Hill. It whistled around the corners of the Valley Grove House. It traveled with a throaty roar through the trees above the hotel, which Bill's mother had started while Bill was away with Lew Simpson.

Bill had passed his fourteenth birthday. Though he was still growing like a weed, he felt like a man. Especially when he got mad at his everlasting wood chopping.

"Don't try to chop all that wood at once,

lad. You'll have nothing to do tomorrow."

Bill knew that crisp voice. It belonged to
Lew Simpson. The boy turned around and put
down his axe. He looked up at the horseman
and grinned a broad grin.

"First day there's nothing to do around
here, I'll grow wings and fly away," Bill said,
laughing. "Light down and rest your saddle,
Lew."

Lew chuckled. "Don't mind if I do, Bill. I
want to powwow with you."

Lew dismounted and they went under the
woodshed out of the wind. Bill leaned back
against the neatly stacked wood, and rested.
Lew sat down near by.

"Bill," he said, "I've got to take a mule train
to Fort Laramie near a thousand miles west of
here. I can't find enough good men to drive
the mules. How'd you like to go along?"

Bill thought a minute. "I don't know, Lew.
Mother'd have to pay a full-time man to do
what I do around here. Besides, she don't want
me to quit school again."

"For forty dollars a month, you can hire a

good man to do your chores," Lew said. "I need a mule skinner, the worst way. I'll pay you fifty dollars."

Bill didn't answer at once. He picked up a piece of stovewood and began slicing off thin shavings.

"What's this I hear about a horseback mail service, Lew?" he said.

"You mean the Pony Express? That's one of Russell's ideas. He aims to move the mail overland from Missouri to California in nine days. They're building relay stations now every fifteen miles or so along the line, where riders can get fresh horses and—"

"How much are they going to pay their riders?" Bill asked.

"Big wages, son. A hundred to a hundred and fifty a month, depending on the man."

Bill whistled. "That's for me," he said, folding up his knife. "Why should I drive—"

"But Bill, they ain't even started yet! We can get to Fort Laramie before they do."

"All right," Bill said. "If I can get a good man to help Mother, and persuade her to let

[*133*]

me quit school, I'll go with you. If I can get a job with the Pony Express when we get to Laramie, I'll take it. You can always pick up a mule skinner there."

"It's a deal, Bill," Lew agreed.

Nearly two months later, the mule train drew up outside Fort Laramie and made camp. It was wild country—rugged, barren, and vast. The sun was setting behind the Laramie Mountains. Upriver, a band of antelopes filed down into the canyon to drink. A hunter rode in with a pack train bringing meat for the fort. Indians galloped back and forth over the plains.

As the sun dropped below the rim of the mountains, the ringing notes of a cavalry bugle sounded colors. The flag fluttered down its staff, and night shut in on the lonesome fort.

Around the campfire that night, Lew Simpson said, "Jack Slade's in charge of this district, Bill. He's a tough one. If he don't give you a job with the Pony, remember, you've still got a job with me."

Bill grinned. "Thanks, Lew."

[*134*]

The next morning, just after Lew and the mule train pulled out, Bill saw a dark man on a tall bay horse ride out through the gate of the fort. He figured it was Slade from the descriptions he'd heard of him.

Bill went over to him and the rider halted.

"Are you Captain Slade?" Bill asked, pulling a letter from his pocket.

"I am," Slade said shortly.

"Here's a letter to you from Mr. William Russell," Bill said, passing him the letter.

Slade read it. He held it in his hand and looked Bill over from toe to topknot. His face clouded.

"Young man," he said, "don't think for a minute you're going to ride Pony just because you've got a letter from William Russell saying you're good!"

"I don't," Bill said, looking Slade straight in the eye. "Mr. Russell told me it would be up to you."

"He was right! In the first place, you're too young. It takes men to ride this route."

Bill continued to look him straight in the

[*135*]

eye. "I've been riding ever since I was big enough to shinny up a stirrup strap," he said. "Try me."

A hint of a smile lifted the corners of Slade's lips. "All right," he agreed. "We'll give you a

shot at it. I'm sure goin' to need all the riders I can get. But don't start crying when the going gets tough. And don't blame me if you come in some day stuck full of Indian arrows."

Captain Slade told Bill about the route he was to cover. It was seventy-six miles long. The

[*136*]

eastern station was Red Butte, the western end was at Three Crossings.

"Platte Bridge is the station east of Red Butte," Slade said. "When it's time for the rider with the mail to arrive from there, you have your horse saddled and be outside the Red Butte station.

"Each rider's allowed two minutes to get the mail on his horse and get going. Do it in less if you can. You'll change horses at Willow Springs Station, at Sweetwater, Devil's Gate, and Split Rock."

The mail was carried in a handy mochila. This was a sort of leather blanket with holes in it that fitted over the saddle. On each corner of the blanket was a leather box to carry the mails in. These boxes were very strong and were fitted with stout padlocks. Often there were many thousands of dollars' worth of mail in those pouches.

Bill found riding the Pony Express very exciting. First there would be a streak of dust, next the horse and rider growing larger. Then the rataplan of galloping hoofs, the last burst

[*137*]

of speed, and the squeak of saddle leather.

A station man would be holding the reins of Bill's horse as the rider approached. The newcomer would be out of the saddle before

his pony had stopped. Bill would grab the mochila, throw it on his pony, take the reins from the station man, hop aboard and be on his way.

[*138*]

Seventy-six miles a day! Most of it at high speed. It was a real day's work, but Bill loved it.

Even though he was used to hard work, it

took him awhile to get hardened in to the Pony route. But in two weeks he was thinned down to whalebone and whang-leather.

Bill had such fun that he hardly thought

[*139*]

about danger. One day he was galloping along through a steep-sided valley. He was thinking how fine it was to be part of an outfit that was moving the U. S. Mails almost two thousand miles in nine days. Suddenly his keen eyes caught sight of a little spot of color. It was in a notch of the high rim of hills on his left. And it was not part of nature.

Before most people would have seen it at all, Bill knew that it was the painted feather of an Indian on the warpath. He pretended that he had not noticed anything. Gradually he speeded up his horse until he was in rifleshot of the hidden Indian.

Then he suddenly leaned down along the side of his pony for cover, and swerved off the trail. As he turned, he heard the plunk of a bullet. This was followed by the crack of a rifle, and a puff of smoke floated up from the rim. If he hadn't swerved, the bullet would have hit him.

Bill galloped on. Naked, painted Indian riders came plunging down the slope ahead of him. Shrill war cries shattered the silence of the canyon.

*Shrill war cries shattered the silence
of the canyon*

Bill drew his revolver and thumbed back the hammer. His horse traveled like a streak of light.

Luckily for Bill, the Indians ahead had no rifles. As they rode, they fitted arrows to their bowstrings. They were not quite down to the trail when Bill came opposite them. He raised his revolver. One Indian was about to let go his drawn-back bowstring. Bill fired.

The Indian sagged in the saddle. His arrow fluttered weakly to the ground. Then Bill was through the valley gate and going like the wind. A shower of feathered death whizzed around him.

Though the Indian horses were good, they couldn't keep up with Bill's swift Express pony. The next relay station was Three Crossings. It wasn't far off. By the time Bill pulled his heaving, sweat-soaked horse up in front of it, the redskins had given up the chase.

He was glad that Three Crossings was the end of his route. He'd have time to eat and to rest and to tell about the Indian attack, before starting back for Red Butte. He looked around for the rider who was to carry the mail on.

[142]

A saddled horse was tied to the corral fence, but there was no one in sight except the station tender.

"Hey, Sam, where's the rider?" Bill asked, swinging himself from his saddle.

"We had a little party here last night," Sam said. "He got mad at something and one of the boys had to shoot him."

"Is he hurt too bad to ride?" Bill asked.

"I reckon so. He's dead."

That meant that Bill had to go on to Rocky Ridge, eighty-four miles farther west. Hastily he swallowed some water. He put his mochila on the fresh horse. While Sam hung a canteen of water on his saddle, he mounted. Sam handed him up a juicy hump-rib of buffalo meat. And Bill made off, chewing on it. He'd need the strength it would give him, before he was through.

Bill was beginning to feel that this was no fun. On and on he rode, relaxing to the swing of the horse as best he could. He changed at St. Mary's, and again at Rock Creek. He went over South Pass, and down into the Great Salt Lake Basin.

He crossed a creek at the Big Sandy Swing Station, and another at Dry Sandy, and from there turned south along Green River. At Rocky Ridge he met the rider from the west. He took the mochila and headed east again.

Bill met no more Indians on this trip. But he was one tired boy, half asleep in his saddle, when he pulled in and lifted his aching leg over the saddle at Red Butte. He had covered about three hundred and twenty miles. He had tired out twenty-one ponies. And he had been in the saddle twenty-one hours.

This was one of the three longest rides ever made by a Pony Express rider. Never again did anyone question Bill Cody's ability to do a man's work on the trail.

Bill rode the Pony Express till after the Civil War started. By that time men were stringing up telegraph wires in the West. The Pony Express would not be needed much longer. Bill was restless to get into the war. He was still too young to join the army.

"But I'll get into it as soon as I can," he told himself. He quit his job and headed for home.

[*144*]

CHAPTER THIRTEEN

Tough for Buffalo

G IDDAP, Brigham, giddap!"

Bill Cody's heart was not in the command. He didn't like the work he was doing.

Neither did Brigham. No one would think the poky-looking horse pulling the steel scraper was a top-notch buffalo hunter.

But anyone who saw Bill Cody might guess at once that he had been an army scout, because of his long hair, his riding boots, and his buckskin clothes. They'd wonder, though, what he was doing now, all dust and sweat, moving dirt with a scraper.

Half asleep in the blinding Kansas sun, Bill let his mind wander back over the last seven years. As soon as he was old enough, he had joined the Union Army and fought in two battles.

After the war he'd got married. For a while he had run his mother's old hotel in Salt Creek Valley. But the country was building up fast.

A steady stream of wagons filled with settlers

was rolling west. Great herds of Texas long-horns were pushing north.

All this had made the Indians restless. The coming of the white men meant the end of the buffalo. And the buffalo provided the red men with almost everything they used.

The buffalo meat was their main food. The skins made robes and blankets to keep warm. With the hair scraped off, the hides covered Indian tepees. Buffalo horns made strong bows

Without the buffalo, the age-old Indian way of life would end. Some of the Indians had tried to be peaceful. But some of the white men had broken treaties and raided Indian villages, killing all the braves, squaws, and papooses.

[147]

At last even the peaceful Indians had begun to fight back. They had attacked wagon trains. They had killed men working on the railroads. They had raided settlements.

The Army had needed scouts to help keep the Indians in order. And Bill Cody had been one of the best. He had liked scouting. But he had needed more money for his wife and child than he could earn as a scout. So he had given it up.

He had taken a job with the Kansas Pacific Railroad to help lay tracks to the west. Now he was grading a roadbed. And his heart was not in his work. With a sigh, he looked east at the oncoming rails flashing back the blazing sun. He looked west over the endless prairie. There in the distance buffalo were grazing. A band of antelopes were showing their white tail-flags as they fled from some enemy along the river.

Bill looked at them longingly. Grading track might be good for some, but for him it was slavery. Just the same, he was no quitter. As long as sticking was best for his family, he'd stick.

He turned Brigham and headed back toward the cut. Coming toward him was a man in store clothes riding a tall black horse.

Bill knew him. He was one of the Goddard brothers who had a contract to supply meat to the railroad builders.

Bill stopped his scraper. The man pulled up beside him.

"Hello, Cody," he said. "Do you want a better job than the one you've got? I'm hiring buffalo hunters."

Bill took off his hat and wiped the sweat from his forehead. He looked up at the man on the tall horse, with relief in his eyes.

"That sounds good to me," he said. "How much you paying?"

"Five hundred dollars a month—bed, board, and bullets."

"That shines to me!" Bill said.

"Don't make up your mind too fast, Bill," said Goddard. "We're not paying those wages for just sitting on horseback and shooting at buffalo."

"I s'pose not. Is it on account of the

[*149*]

Injuns being riled up the way they are?"

"Right. They're building up a special grudge against the railroad. Gangs are being attacked a hundred miles apart. The Overland Stage won't move without a guard. And especially the Indians hate buffalo hunters."

"That's no news to me," Bill said.

"We've got it fixed with the soldiers in Fort Hays," Goddard went on. "If any hunters are attacked they can send up a smoke signal and the soldiers will come a-running."

Bill nodded. "When do I start?" he asked.

"Soon as you can. We're feeding twelve hundred men. Each of our hunters has got to kill twelve buffaloes a day. We send out a man in a wagon with each hunter, to butcher and bring in the meat."

"Fair enough," said Bill.

He felt free as a bird as he reached down and unhooked Brigham from the scraper. The horse heaved a great sigh. Probably he was even more glad to be free than his master.

The next morning Bill rode out on his new job. The squeak of the saddle was music to his ears. The smell of leather was good in his nostrils. His spirits were as high as the wide, blue prairie sky.

Rattling along behind him came the meat wagon, driven by a blocky man with curly black hair, named Scotty.

Five miles out of camp, Bill began to see black dots in the distance. He opened up his lungs and let out a long-drawn Indian war whoop.

Soon the black dots thickened to a compact herd of buffalo grazing toward the west. As he approached they quickened their pace. Pushed

Bill kept the snorting black mass going in a circle

by the animals in the rear, those in front broke into a trot.

Now Bill's long frontier training came into play.

He gave the speedy Brigham his head. Together they passed the surging ocean of shaggy-humped beasts on the right, and came up to the leader of the herd.

Bill had a breech-loading Springfield rifle that shot a bullet half an inch wide. He rode close to the plunging leader, forcing it to the left.

The beast gave a nasty sideswipe with a short, powerful horn. Brigham dodged. Bill kicked the buffalo in the nose. It looked angrily up at him with its small red eyes.

By this time Bill had the herd running in a circle to the left. He lifted his rifle. Aiming down, and just behind the shoulder, he fired.

The animal swerved. He started gasping for breath, and bleeding from the mouth and nose. Presently he toppled to the ground and the herd went over him.

Bill kept the snorting black mass going in a circle. Every time one broke off in a straight line, trying to escape, Bill shot it. In no time at all he had his day's kill of twelve.

He pulled off to one side. Gradually the herd stopped circling, quieted down, and went to grazing again not far off.

Scotty came up in the meat wagon. "By gum," he said as he pulled his four mules to a stop. "That's the slickest, quickest job of killing meat I ever see."

Bill laughed. "It's a lot better than chasing them all over the prairie at that," he said.

He helped Scotty skin the buffaloes, cut up the meat, and then load the wagon.

Day after day Bill Cody and Scotty went out and came back with their wagonload of meat.

Sometimes they brought in more than the meat from twelve buffaloes. If one hunter was short, or there were more men to feed, Bill would make up the difference. Because he was always able to come home with enough meat he became a hero to the railroad workers. Before he came on the job they had sometimes gone hungry.

But the Indians were getting more and more

troublesome. Seven men of a grading party twenty miles east of Hays City were killed. Soon after, there were several attacks west of the town.

Bill Cody and Scotty were returning one day to camp with a wagonload of meat. This time Bill was not riding Brigham. The fine horse was resting in the corral at Hays City.

They were moving along at a good pace on the open prairie. Bill's bull voice was opened up in a buffalo hunting song, and Scotty was singing along on the high notes.

Suddenly a band of Indians rode up out of the head of a canyon and headed at wind-whistling speed toward the traveling butcher shop.

Bill's horse was good. He might have beaten the redskins to camp. But Scotty and the wagon couldn't go that fast.

Bill saw the Indians first. Singing or not, he was ever watchful.

"Hold it, Scotty! Injuns!" he yelled.

Scotty pulled back the brake handle hard and reined to a quick stop. Bill was off his horse in an instant and tying him to a wagon wheel.

While Scotty unhitched the mules and tied them to another wheel, Bill began throwing the heavy hindquarters of buffalo meat to the ground.

Scotty started stacking them between the wagon wheels. Bill tossed all the heavy hunks of meat out of the wagon. Then he stood up in the wagon bed. He brought his rifle to his shoulder and took a snap shot at the whooping horsemen.

The leader tumbled off his paint pony. Two riders on either side of him leaned down, grabbed his arms, and dragged him away.

The rest of the attackers swerved off and began to circle the two buffalo hunters. Bill and Scotty were very well forted up now, and

had quite a lot of ammunition. They lay under the wagon behind their meaty breastworks. Whenever the Indians shot, they ducked down. At every lull they laid their rifle barrels on the hump meat, and made things hot for the Indians.

Soon both mules were dead and the humps and hindquarters of meat were stuck full of arrows. But Bill and Scotty had brought down five Indians.

The warriors drew off for a powwow. This was more than they had bargained for.

Bill crawled out from under the wagon. He snaked out a little way on the down-wind side. He took a swift glance to see no Indian was aiming at him. Then he pulled a block of sulphur matches from his pocket. He scraped one alongside the leg of his buckskins, and when it had fizzed into flame, set fire to the prairie.

Luckily it was August, and the grass was dry. The flames spread fast. The smoke from the greasy buffalo grass rose thickly.

This was a signal to the soldiers at Fort Hays. Within half an hour a troop of blue-clad cavalry came in sight. The Indians saw them and made off.

The troopers drew their long, straight sabers and came charging down. They swept past the meat wagon, shouting like Saturday night.

But the Indians had too much of a head

start. The cavalry came riding back on blowing horses.

Bill and Scotty had taken the harness off their dead animals and were throwing the meat back in the wagon.

"Looks like someone's going to have a mess of feathers for supper," the captain laughed.

"They'll eat them and like them," Bill answered.

"That's a fact," Scotty piped up. "They near lost their best buffalo hunter today."

Six troopers tied picket ropes to the wagon tongue, and headed for Hays City at a fast trot.

When they got there it was past suppertime. The whole railroad gang, as well as everyone else in the wild town, was gathered in the town square.

They were cheering and waving their hats. A man jumped up on a pile of railroad ties. As Bill rode by, the man shouted:

"Buffalo Bill, Buffalo Bill
Never missed and never will.
Always aims and shoots to kill,
And the company pays his Buffalo Bill.

[*159*]

"Yaa-hoo-ooo!" he yelled. Laughing, he began to repeat the poem. Others took it up till the whole camp was chanting it in rhythm.

They pulled Bill off his horse and carried him about on their shoulders, still reciting it.

The Buffalo Bill name stuck. A few years later almost every boy and girl in America knew that verse by heart. And Buffalo Bill Cody was famous on both sides of the Atlantic.

CHAPTER FOURTEEN

"Buffalo Bill's Wild West"

THE brown house-boards of North Platte, Nebraska, were cracking under a hot August sun. Buffalo Bill Cody stepped out of the bank. His strong eyes swept the dusty street of the prairie town.

On the other side of the street a boy about ten years old was untying a horse from the hitch-rack. It was Brown Jug, Bill's favorite horse. Bill started angrily across the street. But the boy led Brown Jug away from the hitch-rack, and came toward him.

Bill waited. The boy came up and passed him the bridle reins. He looked up at Bill as if he thought he was the most wonderful man in the world.

[*161*]

Bill took the reins and swung up into the saddle

Bill smiled. "Thank you, son," he said.

Wide-eyed, the chunky lad tried to speak, but his throat tied up so, he couldn't.

"What's your name?" Bill asked.

"Johnny Baker," the boy managed to blurt out.

Bill took the reins and swung up into the saddle. As he rode out of town he thought about the look in Johnny's eyes. He knew that Johnny admired him not just because he was Buffalo Bill Cody. But because Johnny was thinking about the frontier West, where Bill had had so many exciting adventures.

Suddenly Bill knew he would like to make millions of people feel as Johnny did about the West. He would like to take the West, East. He would like to start the show he'd dreamed of when he was a boy.

Since his buffalo-hunting days, much had happened to Bill Cody. He had gone back to scouting for the Army again. And he had done so well that General Sheridan had made him Chief of Scouts of the Fifth Cavalry.

His fame as a buffalo hunter and scout had

spread. Books had been written about his life and adventures. Finally, he had been persuaded to become an actor in western plays. At that work he had made a fortune.

He owned a big cattle ranch now. And he had built a home for his family, at North Platte, which he called Scout's Rest. In North Platte he was a leading citizen, always ready to lend a helping hand to people in trouble.

The railroads had crossed the country at last. The buffalo were almost all killed off. The Indians were no longer a threat.

The frontier was tamed. But still Bill craved excitement. Ranching and town life he found dull. He had never really liked acting, though it had made him money. But he had always wanted to run a show. Well, now he would do it! He would get up a show about the pioneer West.

He talked it over with a friend named Nate Salsbury. Nate was a great showman. He believed as strongly as Bill Cody did that a Wild West show would go over like a storm.

This show was to be the real thing. Every act

would give an honest picture of frontier life.
The actors would be people who had lived it.

"Can you get Indians?" Salsbury asked.

"I can get Indians all right, and their war
ponies."

"How about buffaloes?"

"Can do. Buffalo, elk, antelope. Anything
you want, Nate. Maybe even grizzly bear."

"Cowboys?"

"The real thing," Bill replied.

"Buckers?"

"The worst in the West . . . and say, Nate! There's the Deadwood Coach. It went from Laramie to the Black Hills gold diggings in the old days. I know where it's sitting beside the road. No one wants it. It was held up by highwaymen and attacked by Injuns more times than you can count."

"Good. We'll have it attacked in the show," Nate said.

"We'll have lots of kids in the act. They can ride in the coach and be captured."

Salsbury had pencil and paper out and was making a list.

"What else?"

"Mexican fancy ropers," Bill went on. "Steer throwing. Prairie schooners. Bull-trains—"

"What about the Pony Express?" Nate asked.

"Of course. And I can get men who really rode it. Maybe even Pony Bob Haslam . . . I tell you, Nate, there's no end to it."

The two men sat late. Their idea for a brand-new kind of show grew and grew with every minute they talked.

Nate finally said, "It will go like a prairie fire."

Bill went back to Nebraska to get together the animals and the people they would need. It was a big job. By the time the buffalo and other animals were rounded up, and the cowboys and Indians were hired, months had passed.

Meanwhile Bill and little Johnny Baker had become good friends. And as soon as Johnny discovered what his hero was up to, he begged to go along with the show.

Warmhearted Bill Cody couldn't say no. Johnny was so full of happiness, he thought he'd burst.

When the frontiersmen, Indians, cowboys, and livestock were all sure of their acts, the show was ready. It crackled with action.

In May, 1884, the show played in St. Louis for the first time. At their second stop, in Chicago, they played to 41,448 people. In New York, thousands of people jammed into the Polo Grounds to see the show. The whole East rocked and roared with praise of · "Buffalo Bill's Wild West."

It had all worked out as Bill Cody and Nate Salsbury had planned. What a cast of Western characters they had! Every girl and boy from eight to eighty, it seemed, wanted to see them.

John Nelson, who had married an Indian, was in charge of the Indian camp. His six handsome half-Sioux children rode with him on top of the Deadwood Coach when it was attacked. His long whiskers streamed over his shoulders, and the kids screamed in make-believe fear and real delight.

Major Frank North led the Pawnees in their war dance.

Buck Taylor was in charge of the cowboys. He was pushing seven feet tall. He could throw a steer by the horns or tail, and tie him single-handed. He was a wizard with a lasso rope, and could ride the worst bucker in the world.

The other cowboys were almost a match for him in everything but size.

Captain Bogardus, world champion pigeon shot, had his three young sons with him in his act. Edward, fourteen, Peter, twelve, and Henry, ten, were all crack shots.

[168]

Johnny Baker, now known as "The Cowboy Kid," was practicing hard, and would soon be among the world's best marksmen.

It was a great summer. Bill Cody worked himself to the bone, and it paid off.

But no man's string of luck lasts forever. The summer had gone so well that Salsbury and Cody planned to take the show south for the winter.

"We'll go down the Mississippi by boat and give shows in towns along the river to pay our traveling expenses," Nate said. "Then we'll wind up at New Orleans."

"Right," Bill agreed. "I'll go ahead to New Orleans to make arrangements for the show there. And we'll let Pony Bob Haslam arrange for transportation."

"Right," said Nate. And so their plans were made.

Now, though Pony Bob was a good judge of horseflesh, he didn't know much about steamboats. But the tub he hired in Cincinnati managed to carry the animals and the actors from one stop to another along the river. It was rain-ing hard when they finished their last act before taking off for New Orleans.

Bedraggled, and dripping water, the great show boarded the boat in the late afternoon.

It was all that the cowboys, Mexican *vaqueros*, and Indians could do to get the tame,

wild, and half-wild stock loaded onto the boat. The local people came down to the river-

[*170*]

bank, to watch them load. They thought no stranger sight had ever been seen since Noah's Ark.

Broncos, antelopes, elk, deer, bear, and burros were led, herded, or driven across the creaking gangplank.

The prairie schooners, the Deadwood Coach, and the bandwagon were put aboard.

The buffalo were the last to go. The cowboys stood by to help out if they gave trouble, but old Buffalo John had charge of the herd.

Buffalo John was a mystery man. He was an old buffalo hunter. He kept to himself, and never talked much to anybody. But he seemed to know the language of his animals.

The lead buffalo snorted at the gangplank. The whole herd was red-eyed and restless. Everyone was afraid they were going to turn back and stampede.

But old John talked to them. His voice seemed to soothe the shaggy beasts. The gangplank bent like thin ice as they went across, but they made it.

By the time all was stowed away, it was dark. The stamping of hoofs and munching of hay made a muffled sound between the decks. The odor of hot and steaming livestock was a comfortable smell to those who were used to it.

The steamboat backed away into the thick, rainy night. Her foghorn sounded hoarsely. Then—*crash!* She backed right into another steamer heading into the dock.

The shock of the crash threw the show people to the deck. The sound of splintering wood was followed by a swirling rush of muddy water through the ship. Buffaloes bellowed. Horses neighed for help. The steamboat sank quickly. The people barely had time to get out alive.

They struggled ashore, and then went to work trying to save what they could.

But when they took stock next morning, they found that, except for a few horses, every animal had drowned. And all the equipment was lost except the Deadwood Coach and the bandwagon.

CHAPTER FIFTEEN

"World by the Tail!"

BUFFALO BILL CODY sat on his tall white horse outside the arena of the Wild West Show. He was giving his troupers a last inspection as they lined up for the grand review.

He had brought the show to England. This was a command performance, ordered by Queen Victoria herself.

She would be there with half the royalty of Europe, for this was the fiftieth year of her rule. All England was celebrating.

"No slip-ups today," thought Bill. "Everything's got to be right with the Queen watching."

Nate Salsbury came out of the arena and stood beside him.

"There's 40,000 people out there," he said. "Every seat is taken. Does that make you happy?"

"Happy? I'm as happy as the sun! We've got the world by the tail with a downhill drag!"

Joy was in Bill's powerful voice, and in the smile that spread over his face.

"We've come a long way, haven't we?" Salsbury said.

"That's a fact, partner," Bill agreed. "It's a long, long way from herding cows at twenty-five dollars a month."

His mind flashed back to the sad nine-year-old boy going to work after his father's death. He wished Isaac Cody could be here today.

Bill's piercing eyes swept over the outfit. Everything was in order. And his heart was brimful of pride at the sight of the colorful display.

He was proud, too, when he remembered how the outfit had stuck by him after that terrible shipwreck on the Mississippi.

Rebuilding the show in time to open on schedule in New Orleans was the hardest job Bill had ever tackled. But he'd done it.

Even then his troubles hadn't ended. Weeks

of rain, rain, and more rain kept people away from the show in droves. One day the ticket man plowed through the mud and drizzle to Bill's tent.

"We'd better call off the show today," he said gloomily. "There's only nine people in the audience."

"Did they pay to get in?" Bill asked.

"Yes."

"Well, if nine people came out here in all this rain to see us, we'll show," said Cody.

But there had been one bright spot in that dark winter in New Orleans. Bill would never forget the day Frank Butler and his wife had come looking for a job. They were a shooting team. And they were working for a circus that was treating them badly.

Frank said, "We hear this is a good outfit to work with. We'd like a chance."

"They tell us the 'Bill Show' is just like a big family," his slim little wife added with a smile.

"All right," Cody agreed. "I'll give you a try."

He handed his own rifle to the buckskin-clad

[*176*]

girl. The moment her hand touched the gun Bill felt a thrill. He sensed that she was something special.

Now, Bill beamed a broad smile at her as she sat waiting on her horse.

"The greatest trick shot the world has ever known," he thought. "My luck sure changed when Annie Oakley joined this show."

Bill's eyes turned from Annie Oakley to some of the other young troupers. How well they had proved their worth to the show!

There were the handsome papooses of John Nelson. They were sitting on top of the old Deadwood Stagecoach.

[*177*]

"Cody," he'd whispered to himself, *"you've fetched 'em!"*

Bill looked for Lillian Smith of California. She was good with the rifle, too. At the age of seven, little Lillian had shot a wildcat out of the high limbs of a redwood tree. Yes, there she was, all dressed up and ready to work.

And there were the riders. Buck Taylor, "King of the Cowboys," towered over them. They were great boys, every one of them. They could ride anything they could get a leg across. And the horses were real buckers.

"In fact," thought Bill proudly, "there's nothing fake in the whole show."

There were the Indians, fresh from the West, a hundred of them. The first day they had appeared here in England, the Prince of Wales had been in the audience. When a hundred Indians, mounted on many-colored war ponies, had torn into the arena from ambush, the Prince had leaped to his feet with shining eyes.

Bill had been near by and had seen it. "Cody," he'd whispered to himself, "you've fetched 'em!"

He surely had. Prince Edward's report to

*"Allow me to present the greatest Scout
of the West—Buffalo Bill!"*

the Queen had led to this command performance.

Now it was time to start. Bill heard the voice of Frank Richmond, the announcer. The band struck up a lively tune.

A group of riders went through the entrance. The clopping of their hoofs echoed from the sides of the arena. They loped rapidly to the far end and lined up. Another group went in, and another, till at last each section of the show was waiting silently.

Then a single figure on a tall white horse came through the entrance. His long hair flowed over his shoulders. Mustache and goatee pointed up his face. He rode tall and straight, with the easy swing of a man who lives in the saddle. He guided the spirited horse to the center of the arena without effort.

Richmond, the announcer, introduced him:

"Ladies and Gentlemen. Allow me to present the greatest Scout of the West—Buffalo Bill!"

The rider wheeled his prancing horse in front of the Queen. He brought him to a quick

[181]

stop that lifted him up on his hind feet. Amid a tumult of approving shouts and hand clapping, he let the horse down and waited for quiet.

Then he swept off his big sombrero. The white horse bowed low. This brought more applause. When it stopped, Buffalo Bill's deep voice soared over the grandstands:

"Ladies and Gentlemen. Permit me to introduce to you—THE WILD WEST!"

A boy's dream had come true.

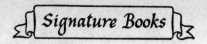

"Names That Made History"

ENID LAMONTE MEADOWCROFT, *Supervising Editor*

THE STORY OF ANDREW JACKSON
    By Enid LaMonte Meadowcroft. *Illustrated by David Hendrickson*
THE STORY OF THOMAS JEFFERSON
    By Earl Schenck Miers.   *Illustrated by Reynold C. Pollak*
THE STORY OF JOAN OF ARC
    By Jeannette Covert Nolan.   *Illustrated by Pranas Lapé*
THE STORY OF JOHN PAUL JONES
    By Iris Vinton.   *Illustrated by Edward A. Wilson*
THE STORY OF HELEN KELLER
    By Lorena A. Hickok.   *Illustrated by Jo Polseno*
THE STORY OF JACQUELINE KENNEDY
    By Alida Sims Malkus   *Illustrated by Michael Lowenbein*
THE STORY OF PRESIDENT KENNEDY
    By Iris Vinton.   *Illustrated by Carl C. Cassler*
THE STORY OF LAFAYETTE
    By Hazel Wilson.   *Illustrated by Edy Legrand*
THE STORY OF ROBERT E. LEE
    By Iris Vinton.   *Illustrated by John Alan Maxwell*
THE STORY OF ABRAHAM LINCOLN
    By Nina Brown Baker.   *Illustrated by Warren Baumgartner*
THE STORY OF MOZART
    By Helen L. Kaufmann.   *Illustrated by Eric M. Simon*
THE STORY OF FLORENCE NIGHTINGALE
    By Margaret Leighton.   *Illustrated by Corinne B. Dillon*
THE STORY OF ANNIE OAKLEY
    By Edmund Collier.   *Illustrated by Leon Gregori*
THE STORY OF LOUIS PASTEUR
    By Alida Sims Malkus.   *Illustrated by Jo Spier*
THE STORY OF POCAHONTAS
    By Shirley Graham.   *Illustrated by Mario Cooper*
THE STORY OF MARCO POLO
    By Olive Price.   *Illustrated by Federico Castellon*
THE STORY OF ELEANOR ROOSEVELT
    By Lorena A. Hickok.   *Illustrated by William Barss*
THE STORY OF FRANKLIN D. ROOSEVELT
    By Lorena A. Hickok.   *Illustrated by Leonard Vosburgh*
THE STORY OF THEODORE ROOSEVELT
    By Winthrop Neilson.   *Illustrated by Edward A. Wilson*
THE STORY OF ROBERT LOUIS STEVENSON
    By Joan Howard.   *Illustrated by Jo Polseno*
THE STORY OF MARK TWAIN
    By Joan Howard.   *Illustrated by Donald McKay*
THE STORY OF GEORGE WASHINGTON
    By Enid LaMonte Meadowcroft. *Illustrated by Edward A. Wilson*
THE STORY OF MARTHA WASHINGTON
    By Jeannette Covert Nolan.   *Illustrated by Corinne B. Dillon*
THE STORY OF MAD ANTHONY WAYNE
    By Hazel Wilson.   *Illustrated by Lawrence Beall Smith*
